RIDE WITH YOUR MIND
ESSENTIALS

RIDE WITH YOUR MIND
ESSENTIALS

Innovative learning strategies for
basic riding skills

Mary Wanless

TRAFALGAR SQUARE PUBLISHING
North Pomfret, Vermont

First published in the United States of America in 2002 by
Trafalgar Square Publishing, North Pomfret, Vermont 05053

Published simultaneously in Great Britain by
Kenilworth Press, Addington, Buckingham, MK18 2JR

Printed and bound in Spain for Compass Press

ISBN 1-57076-244-9

Library of Congress Control Number: 2002112464

Illustrations by Dianne Breeze (except those on page 67, by Christine Bousfield)
Design by Paul Saunders; layout by Kenilworth Press

Acknowledgements

My thanks go to Lesley Gowers and all at Kenilworth Press, to my illustrator Dianne Breeze, and to Martha Cook and all at Trafalgar Square Publishing.

I also want to thank my team at Overdale Equestrian Centre, especially Sam Twyman and Anna Gordon – they hold the fort for me, give me lots of support, and repeatedly forgive me when I race off saying 'I've just got to go and ...'!

Thanks, guys!

Disclaimer of liability

Contents

PORTIA NELSON

Autobiography in Five Short Chapters

Chapter One
I walk down the street.
There is a deep hole in the sidewalk.
I fall in.
I am lost … I am helpless.
It isn't my fault.
It takes forever to find a way out.

Chapter Two
I walk down the same street.
There is a deep hole in the sidewalk.
I pretend I do not see it.
I fall in again.
I can't believe I am in this same place.
But it isn't my fault.
It still takes a long time to get out.

Chapter Three
I walk down the same street.
There is a deep hole in the sidewalk.
I see it is there.
I fall in … it's a habit … but my eyes are open.
I know where I am.
It is my fault.
I get out immediately.

Chapter Four
I walk down the same street.
There is a deep hole in the sidewalk.
I walk round it.

Chapter Five
I walk down a different street.

Introduction –
How to Use This Book

Learning to ride well is a mammoth task – far larger than most riders realise. But paradoxically, skilful riding is also much more possible than most people's experience suggests. Whilst beginners make rapid progress, most of them become club level riders who are stuck on a plateau despite the investment of time, money, hope, prayer and will-power. If you are willing to 'think outside the box' it need not be this way.

Much of the received wisdom of riding is hearsay, yet most riders act as if those traditional tenets were etched on tablets of stone. Those familiar phrases simply describe feelings that a good rider had one day and then taught to her student, who taught them to her student, who taught them to her student ... and so on, like a giant inter-generational game of 'Chinese Whispers' (also known as 'Telephone'). Somewhere along the line they became generalisations considered good for all riders at all times – rather than helpful pointers for certain people at certain stages in learning.

The meaning of some of them, like 'push' for example, has changed so dramatically over the years that their interpretation has evolved from chalk to cheese. This process has led to a culture of vagueness and misunderstandings, perpetuated and believed by teachers and pupils alike. The chain continues since few people are brave enough to challenge it by asking, 'Exactly what do I push with, and how do I push with it?' (The answer to this is on page 36.) We all know that this level of inquisition might not endear us to our teachers – and their reaction could, of course, cover up the fact that they do not know the answers. Thus the blind keep leading the blind, whilst the small percentage of sighted (or talented) riders cannot untangle the web and teach us all to see.

The horse world is rich in descriptive knowledge that tells us what horse and rider should look like. But traditionally we lack good information about 'how'. Good riders just do it, without knowing how they do it, and without understanding why you are not like them and cannot do it. Furthermore, what they **say** they do may well not match what they **actually** do – hence they can actively maintain the split between popular misinterpretations and their personal embodied (but not necessarily verbal) understanding of riding.

Even when good riders accurately report what they do, what works for them may not work for you, and many of those traditional phrases represent feelings worth aiming for when you are already an accomplished rider. 'Grow up tall and stretch your leg down' is one of these. Good riders usually tell us about the tip of their personal iceberg of skill and have little conception of the enormity of the skill-base that lies beneath the surface of their awareness. What eludes the average rider are the skills that these good riders take for granted and cannot put into words.

It has been my personal mission to uncover this hidden part of the iceberg. During twenty-three years of research I have done everything in my power to expose the secrets of talent, breaking them down into 'bite-size chunks' and finding ways of describing them that work for average riders. The net result is that I and my colleagues can clone good riders. Accomplished riders who are aiming for the top seek my expertise with the 'fatal flaws' that have proved persistent and hard to fix, whilst many club level riders simply want to know that their basics work well enough to prevent them from torturing their horses.

In our work it is as if we give each rider a tool kit, or refine the tool kit that she already has. This 'first tool kit' concerns her body, for its position and texture, its asymmetry, and its stability (or lack of it), affect the horse profoundly. In both you and your horse there are places where movement 'goes through' and places where it is blocked, deadened, dissipated or disorganised. As you affect him and he affects you, the influence of your body mechanics, for good or ill, is enormous – but this is rarely acknowledged. Many trainers, for instance, ignore the rider's way of sitting and think only of teaching her to ride the school movements. These form the rider's 'second tool kit', and when done correctly (from a body that functions well) they undoubtedly have profound training effects. But we cannot afford to negate the exquisite sensitivity that horses have to our body mechanics.

When we riders run out of tools we all resort to shove, kick, pull and pray; but long before this (when there is but a tiny nick in our chisel) we start having negative effects on our horses. They are born with the ability to read us like a book, and they play on our weaknesses, evolving their evasive patterns around the loopholes that we offer them. They **mirror** us, in both our rightness and our wrongness. Also, they know our bottom line – how determined we are, and how little effort we will accept. When **you** change, your horse changes, and you are the key to evasions, limitations and attitudes that many would attribute to him alone. The impact you have on him is far greater than you realise.

Whatever level you ride at or aspire to, coupling this realisation with effective teaching tools turns your riding into a journey of learning and exploration, and this makes it much more fun for both you and your horse. Approaching it like this certainly beats going round and round in circles making the same mistakes, facing the same frustrations, and trying harder in response. As Portia Nelson says so beautifully in her poem, the 'hole in your sidewalk' will not go away, but once you have realised its existence you can begin the process of choosing not to fall in it. From the time that your 'eyes are open' it does not take so long for you to choose to 'walk round it', and ultimately, we can all decide to 'walk down a different street'.

This is an interesting time for my work. In the world of fitness and exercise, core muscle strength is being recognised as an essential component. It is being emphasised particularly in the Pilates system of training, and in work with physioballs (also known as gymnastic balls), and many fitness trainers now believe that it enhances almost any sporting skill. The basis of my message has been that the need to stabilise the body on top of a moving horse demands this strength, and that this is the most basic component of talent. Only now is laboratory research attempting to discover what good riders actually do (as opposed to what they say they do). We will soon know beyond any shadow of doubt that the rider who looks and feels as if she is doing nothing is actually presenting one of the greatest optical illusions of all time.

You may want to read this book straight through to gain an overview of the ideas it presents. When you begin your work with it, go slowly and take time. Be open-minded and curious. Meld a willingness to experiment with a thorough, diligent approach. Remember that this is only the tour guide, just as your teachers are only tour guides. You yourself must take the tour.

It is much less fun to travel alone than with friends, so I hope you will find someone to journey alongside you. Even talking on the telephone or sharing emails can help. But your best companion is a friend with a video camera who will exchange sessions with you, for (alongside your horse) instant visual feedback is your most effective teacher. When you only have your bodily sensations to go by, it is all too easy to con yourself, and the biggest challenge of the learning process is the way that changes always **feel** so much bigger than they **look**. This is just the same phenomenon as getting an ulcer in your mouth or losing a filling, and discovering that what feels to your tongue like a huge great blemish looks in the mirror like a tiny little pin-prick.

To experience the full impact of this, fold your arms, and then unfold them and fold them the other way round. Be sure you have really succeeded, for the old habit is like a 'hole in your sidewalk' that could suck you back into it. This new way of doing it will feel strange – but probably not half so strange as the changes you need to make in your riding.

You do yourself a great disservice when you set limits on how weird you are willing to feel, and many riders are convinced that they have done enough when they have made only 20 per cent of the change they really need. The most recalcitrant would rather fall repeatedly into that same deep hole than experience the 'weirdness' of walking around it. So when you are tempted to argue your case from your kinaesthetic sense of rightness, and to believe your body and not your friend, remember that it is time to call on the objectivity of her video camera. Only when you have become a very accomplished rider can you be reasonably sure that your body will look the way that it feels.

There is another, equally confusing side to the coin, for as you habituate to a new and weird feeling, it ceases to feel so strange. Then, you may be left asking yourself if this is happening simply because your body is habituating to the change, or because you are selling out on the original feeling and not 'going for it' enough. Conversely, if you are 'going for it' with such determination that it is staying equally weird over time, you have probably already hit 'over-kill'. Without objective visual feedback it is hard to (a) become weird enough initially, and (b) keep track of that feeling as it gradually becomes your new norm. So believe your friend's objective diagnosis, and when you are giving feedback remember that **you** are in the objective position, and encourage her to believe you.

Finding a friend to work with may not be easy, however, and the people where you keep your horse may think that you are crazy to embark on this journey; they may ridicule you, and try to get you to stop. Unfortunately, there could be some truth to their criticisms, since you may appear to ride worse before you appear to ride better. During the stage when you are 'between the devil and the deep blue sea' you may both look and feel uncomfortable. But stick with it, and realise that if you succeed in changing your riding significantly for the better, you may upset the status quo in the environment where you keep your horse. You may find that you pay a price for your skills.

If I succeed in inspiring you to move beyond reading this guide so that you actually take the tour, give yourself at least three months before you decide that the scenery is not for you, or that the mountain is too steep to climb. Remember that the foothills are rarely the most interesting part, and that you always have to climb some way before you see the view. I am saying this in the hope that you will be patient if the pay-off is not immediately worth the effort. Your first faltering steps, however, could be life-changing. Be prepared for either possibility.

There is enough material in this book to last you for over two years. It takes you to the stage of riding your horse in carriage in rising trot, and even if you think you know how to do this, you are bound to find some nuances that have escaped you. Given that less than 5 per cent of riders do this (to my eye) really well, there may also be some fundamentals that have escaped you. If this approach captures your interest and excitement, back it up with my other books and videotapes, which also cover sitting trot, canter and lateral work. Even without that additional input, you can extrapolate the information given here into those realms, for all of the principles of rider/horse interaction still hold true. The iceberg is built on the same hidden base, though expanding it into more advanced work requires additional high-precision tools in your tool kit.

Above all, enjoy your horse. If you decide to take this journey, you will learn to speak his language, and as your body becomes able to say it in 'horse' rather than 'human', you will find him instantly more cooperative. He will thank you for finally making sense.

The Basic Position –
Alignment

▪ *Description of the ideal*

Alignment concerns how the body is stacked up. Most people have heard about the ideal shoulder/hip/heel vertical line, but few people pay much attention to this idea. The rider who has it would land on the riding arena on her feet if her horse were taken out from under her by magic. This is obvious in riders from the Spanish Riding School. Like them, riders with good mechanics have their stirrups set at a length which places the thigh bone at about 45° to the ground. This places the calf at a similar angle, and means that the angles in the rider's joints are more closed than most people expect.

Ideally, the rider's heel points back and down towards the horse's hock, but this must be done with the foot just resting in the stirrup rather than pressing. This requires an unusually flexible ankle joint, and it is sufficient for the rider to get the heel level with the toe in this position.

▪ *Common starting points*

Many riders think of having their lower leg 'on the girth' and of keeping their heels down. This commonly results in them sitting in the armchair seat, with their backside behind their feet. This rider is often round-backed, and she rides with a fairly short stirrup, making her thigh bone too horizontal, and placing her knee too high up on the saddle. The tilt of her pelvis leaves her sitting on the back of her buttocks, with her seat bones pointing forward. Riders in this category range from novice riders who are passengers to confident riders who like to ride on trails and jump. It also includes professional riders who bring on young horses and compete. Whilst jumping riders need a shorter stirrup, many exaggerate their position, with their feet too far forward and their pelvis too tucked under them.

Aspiring dressage riders often try to grow up tall and stretch their legs down. They tend to ride with their stirrups too long, and their thigh almost vertical. In order to open the angle between the leg and the torso to this degree, the rider has to hollow her back. The tilt of her pelvis makes her seat bones point back. She also lifts her chest and often her chin, stretching the whole front of her torso and pulling her stomach in. Some riders keep their pelvis reasonably well aligned (instead of sticking their

A beautifully organised rider and horse.

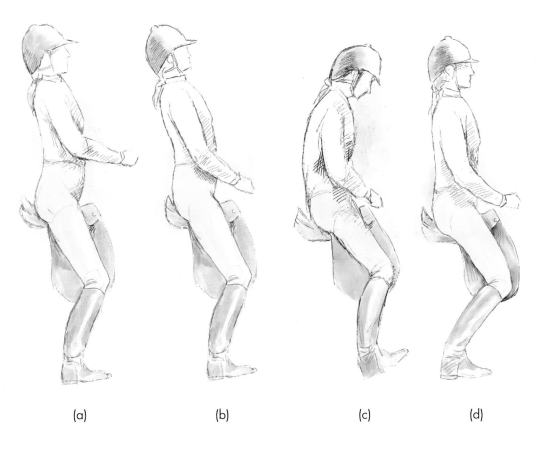

(a) (b) (c) (d)

(a) Hollow-backed rider, has seat bones pointed back, and thighs too vertical.

(b) 'Sophisticated hollow back', often seen in more experienced riders. From the waist, the rider leans back and lifts the chest.

(c) Round-backed rider, whose front is 'C' shaped. Has seat bones pointed forward, thighs rotated out and knee too far up.

(d) Well-aligned rider, seat bones pointed down.

backside out behind them), but then bring their shoulders back from the waist. Their seat bones will usually point forward. Eventually, this posture is likely to lead to back pain. If one compares these riders to a martial artist, it becomes clear that their 'tallness' de-stabilises them and leads to a loss of power. This is rarely recognised in teaching.

Both round- and hollow-backed riders hear the phrase 'push your heel down' and suppose that they should press hard into the stirrups. However, the foot should just **rest** on the stirrup, since pushing down invokes Newton's third law of motion (which states that every action has an equal and opposite reaction). Thus it creates an equal and opposite push **up**, which straightens the knee and hip joints, and sends the rider's backside up and out of the saddle. This explains why so many riders sit to the trot better without their stirrups.

▪ *The fix*

Firstly, diagnose yourself. You need visual feedback to help you decide if you are round- or hollow-backed. If you get this wrong, your work with this book will take you even further up your gum tree!

I always begin realigning the rider by bringing her lower legs up over the front of the saddle so that they rest there. In this position, most people can find their seat bones and get them to point straight down. When you (or better still when a friend) brings down your leg, you need to make sure that the thigh is rotated inwards, with the flesh from the inside of the thigh drawn round to the back. Be sure that you think of the thigh and calf creating an arrowhead shape, where the knee is at the point of the arrowhead. **The knee must be out in front of the hip**, and it is a big mistake to try and bring it back under your hip by making the thigh and calf more vertical.

This is the time to check the length of your stirrups. You may well need to adjust them to bring the thigh bone to 45° to the ground (if you are relatively inexperienced) or slightly more vertical if you are a more established rider. Err on the side of caution, and remember that this change will feel bigger than it looks. Putting your stirrups up just one hole can make you feel as if you have changed from a dressage rider to a jockey, whilst

The angles at the rider's joints, assuming that the thigh bone and calf are the same length, and measuring the hip angle from the thigh bone and not the top of the thigh: (a) more experienced rider; (b) more novice rider.

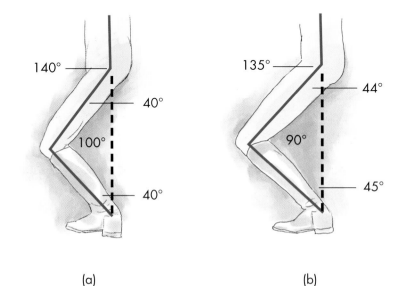

(a)　　　　　　　(b)

Common responses

These vary from:

'This makes the inside and/or the front of my thighs feel like they are being stretched.'

'My thighs, knees and toes are rotated in much more.'

'My feet feel as if they are somewhere way back behind me by the horse's stifles.'

From round-backed riders:

'It's hard to keep my waistband and sternum advancing like this. I keep wanting to give way in my middle.'

'I don't feel safe lined up like this. What if he bucks?'

From hollow-backed riders:

'I feel like the Hunchback of Notre Dame!'

'I'm so slouched and toppling forward, and I can't bear feeling this inelegant.'

to:

'It's as if my brain cannot talk to the middle of my back. It's so hard to get my waistband to come back.'

and:

'At least it doesn't feel so weird any more, but I'm still finding myself reverting to the old way when I'm stressed.'

'So I've over-corrected and gone from rounded to hollow? So now for the next phase ...'

lengthening them one hole can make you feel that your base of support has been eroded. Commonly, people have to alter their stirrup length by two, three and occasionally even four holes, with the majority of riders having to take their stirrups up. Be prepared for the shock, and stick with it, however weird you feel!

Make sure that both stirrups are the same length, and keep them like this even if they do not feel level when you know, objectively, that they actually are. Then be sure that the ball of the foot rests lightly in the stirrup, and that the knobble of the ankle bone lies directly under the bony knobble at the top outside of the thigh.

For round-backed riders – Getting a shoulder/hip/heel vertical line requires you to sit less 'on your pockets' and further forward on your pelvic floor, with your pubic bone closer to the saddle. Your waistband and sternum almost certainly need to be in advance of their normal position, and you may need to feel that you are lifting your chest. The net result has to be that your pubic bone, belly button, sternum and collar bone form a straight vertical line. Advancing your sternum and waistband may feel very stressful, but do not let them drop back. If you find this really difficult, it can help to think of the points of your hips sticking out through your breeches. Keep noticing if your seat bones point down or forwards.

For hollow-backed riders – Your waistband must come back to take the hollow out of your back. This might even make you feel as if you have been punched in the stomach. Your chest will need to drop from its excessively lifted position, and it can help to think of your chest aiming towards the horse's ears (and in some cases even lower). Bringing the body into the posture of a martial artist requires you to feel as if you are becoming short rather than tall. Think of dropping your ribs down towards your hips, and notice that far more of the back of your backside is now down on the saddle. This is a particularly useful landmark. Do your seat bones point down or back? Again, the net result has to be that your pubic bone, belly button, sternum and collar bone form a straight vertical line. Be sure that your collar bone is not behind your sternum. Think of them as a T shape with the bar of the T (the collar bone) directly over the stem of the T (the sternum). This will almost certainly make you feel as if you are leaning forward.

The sensations of being forward, slouched and short will be very disconcerting and you are unlikely to have the courage to venture far enough from your original 'home'. Making these changes profoundly enough will also require you to address your breathing pattern (see Chapter 5). Riders who are 'too tall' usually breathe in their upper chest, and this maintains the lift of their ribcage, along with a top-heaviness and a lack of resilient strength. Learn to drop your ribs and your breathing **down**.

▪ *Troubleshooting – now*

Believe the objective feedback you are getting about your line-up, and keep doing it, however strange it feels! Which of the changes you have made would you most like to sell out on? This will be your downfall.

Remember that unless you are jumping, it is not important to push your heels down – and even then, you must not press hard into the stirrup. Pushing the heel down and forward towards the horse's knee will always cause you to lose your alignment. The ball of your foot must rest (not press) on the stirrup, mirroring the way in which a diver stands on a diving board about to do a backward dive. If your weight goes into your heel you start to dive backwards, and you will have to invoke compensatory strategies to keep your balance. You will either lean back, pull on the reins and 'water-ski', or will forever find yourself tending to fold forward towards 'two-point' and jumping position.

If your reins get too long, your hand will come back towards your body, and then your body will come back. Round-backed riders are particularly vulnerable to this mistake. Keep your reins short enough for your hands to stay out in front of the horse's withers.

▪ *Troubleshooting – on through time*

The concept of aligning the body over seat bones which point straight down sounds very simple, but it is amazingly elusive to many riders. If you manage not to sell out on the idea, you can expect to 'overkill' in a variety of ways before you finally stabilise and find 'home'. The options are leaning forward and back, as well as rounding and hollowing your back. Your lower leg is most likely to stay too far forward, but you may eventually over-correct and bring it too far back.

Keep getting objective visual feedback from friends, photographs, video or mirrors, and adjust accordingly. Remember the golden rule: believe what you see, not what you feel.

▪ *Test yourself – have you got it?*

When the rider is correctly aligned, an observer standing at 90° to her could impose a stick figure on her silhouette. This test sounds far too simple to be true, but it is an extremely useful guide.

Both round-backed and hollow-backed riders need to check that they end up with their seat bones pointing down and a straight vertical line up their front from their pubic bone to their belly button, sternum and collar bone. Monitor this regularly, and keep track of the images or 'feelages' that best help you get there.

If someone placed her fingers between the ball of your foot and the stirrup, would they be screaming? Imagine this as you ride, realising that your weight must be placed **somewhere**, and that the weight that was in your feet must now be taken in your thighs.

▪ *Off-horse exercises*

Sit on your hands, palms down, on a firm chair. Practise moving slowly between the extremes of rounding and hollowing your back, and feel where your seat bones point as you do so. Make the movements smaller and slower until you can distinguish exactly where 'down' is. Notice whether you have an equal range in both directions, or whether rounding or hollowing your back comes more naturally to you. Build up your car seat if necessary so that it becomes a firm, level surface, with a back that supports your spine. Practise sitting with your seat bones pointing straight down, and your back in 'neutral spine'.

Neutral spine is the ideal spinal alignment, in which the spinal curves (which are more or less exaggerated in different people) are balanced. The spine should not be ram-rod straight – it curves forward behind your neck, slightly back between your shoulder blades, forward at your waist, and back at your sacrum. One curve is often more pronounced at the expense of the others, but pointing your seat bones down gives you a first approximation of neutral. If you are struggling with your alignment on or off horse, book a session with a physical therapist or other bodyworker, telling her that neutral spine is your goal. If you have back pain, living, working and riding in this alignment may well keep you pain-free.

Sit on a hard chair with your seat bones pointing down, and your feet resting on the ground. Then press hard into one foot, and notice what happens to the seat bone on that side. It will almost certainly lift. This is Newton's third law in action, demonstrating exactly what happens when you push into the stirrup. Now push on the opposite foot. Does this feel less familiar? If it does, you have demonstrated how you habitually defy gravity on one side of your body, and how strange it feels to do so on the more grounded side. This tendency explains how and why you lose one seat bone, and get a lean and twist in your torso. Welcome to the world of asymmetries! Save this information for later.

Chapter

The Essential Connection – Seat Bones

■ *Description of the ideal*

Skilled riders can feel their seat bones as they ride, and know exactly where they are and where they are pointing, but they are not so weighted that they become like stiletto heels digging into the horse's back. Their torso remains stacked up over their seat bones in neutral spine, and the seat bones form their primary connection with the horse.

■ *Common starting points*

Most riders tend to be either round- or hollow-backed, and thus to point their seat bones either forward or back. Few people realise how important it is to align the pelvis so that the seat bones point down. How easy they are to feel is dictated by the amount and the texture of the flesh in each rider's backside, and how her weight is distributed between her backside, thighs and stirrups. Some riders have very little flesh beneath their seat bones, and are likely to take too much of their weight on these bony knobbles. Other riders have **so much** flesh between their seat bones and the

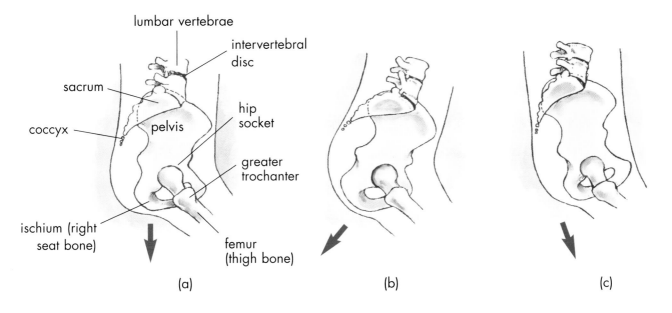

lumbar vertebrae

intervertebral disc

sacrum

hip socket

coccyx

pelvis

greater trochanter

ischium (right seat bone)

femur (thigh bone)

(a)

(b)

(c)

saddle that they struggle to find them. The muscles in this area are often held so tightly that the rider 'pops herself up' and takes her seat bones even more out of contact with the saddle.

Pressing hard into the stirrups is another way of making the seat bones harder to feel, as it straightens the knee and the hip joints, sending the backside and seat bones up off the saddle. Yet another way is tightening the muscles of the pelvic floor, as you would if you were to stop yourself from peeing or poo-ing. (I am sorry to be so blunt, but this pattern causes riders such grief that it is worth mentioning.)

(a) Pelvis well placed, seat bones point down, spine in its neutral position.

(b) Hollow-backed rider, sits towards the pubic bone with seat bones pointing back.

(c) Round-backed rider, sits 'on pockets' with seat bones pointing forward.

■ *The fix*

If you have difficulty feeling your seat bones – be sure that you let go of the muscles between your seat bones and the saddle. Practise tightening up and letting go, until the difference is really clear to you. It may help to sit on your hands as you do this. After the hand, arm and shoulder girdle, these 'pop up' muscles are the next muscle group which likes to get involved when it should not do so. Keep catching yourself when you tighten up, and keep letting the muscles go, being sure that you can feel your seat bones and that they point straight down. Be sure too that you could pee and you could poo. (If your doctor has prescribed Kegel exercises, do

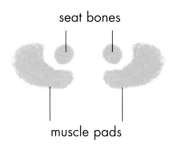

seat bones

muscle pads

The shape made by your underneath when you have both the seat bone and the pad.

them off horse but never when riding.)

If you cannot find one or both seat bones despite all your best efforts, lift one knee and foot a little, bringing your knee away from the saddle. The seat bone on that side should appear through your flesh. Now you have to work out how you can drop your leg back into place and keep your seat bone on the saddle. It is very common for one seat bone to be easier to feel than the other, and whilst you can and should do your best to even them out, this will not be resolved until we look directly at issues of asymmetry.

If you have extremely bony seat bones, or once you have mastered the above: from a state of being maximally 'let go', gradually begin to tighten the muscles under your backside. You should feel the tightening begin to the outside of each seat bone, creating a pad of muscle in a quadrant of a circle that reaches towards the back of the seat bone. You may not be able to tighten very much before the pad moves in under the seat bone and pops you up. Once you reach this point you have gone too far. Let go, start

Common responses

These vary from:

'Every time I try to do something else, I pop up at the same time! It's driving me nuts.'

to:

'This is finally becoming less of a big deal. At least I have something between being completely "let go" or being completely "popped up". I'm much more aware of my underneath and what it's doing, and I can keep it right more of the time.'

and:

'I'm so glad that I don't get sore on my seat bones any more. I have a really butch muscle pad now, and can firm it up so much more without popping up.'

again, and attempt to stop at the point when you have both the pad to the outside of the seat bone, **and** the seat bone itself.

If you are extremely bony, learning to hold the muscle like this gives you a much larger base of support and takes the pressure off your seat bones. If you began by being too 'popped up', be sure that you have gone through the stage of learning to let go before you begin this second stage. This takes some practice, and initially you will find yourself with either the seat bones and no pad, or with a pad and no seat bones. Over time you will find that the muscle which forms the pad becomes bigger and stronger, and that you can firm it up more without popping yourself up. During one to two years of practice your backside will change shape, and it will become virtually impossible for you to pop yourself up.

▪ *Troubleshooting – now*

Do the dismounted exercise below, and take time to discover how much holding is 'just right'. Keep checking that your seat bones still point down rather than forward or back. The two most important variables are where they point, and how your flesh is arranged between being completely 'let go', popping up, and having the muscle pad to the outside and back of each seat bone. If you are a very 'let go' (i.e. low-tone) person, you may do better being too 'popped up' than completely 'let go', but keep attempting to identify and ingrain the ideal.

You now have enough information to make yourself a checklist of things to remember as you ride. Try to keep the list to manageable proportions, and keep cycling through it, giving yourself just short reminders of the most pertinent points.

▪ *Troubleshooting – on through time*

The placing of the seat bone and the pad has more importance than you can realise right now, so keep noticing what is happening, and appreciate that you are likely to 'overkill' and pop up at some stage. You are also likely to go from being too round-backed to too hollow-backed, or vice versa.

When you are hacking out, use the time to notice your pelvic organisation and your alignment. This is valuable time for ingraining these changes, so don't waste it by 'tuning out'. When you are in the arena, get feedback regularly from an external source. (Even non-riders can be trained to tell you if your pubic bone, belly button, sternum and collar bone are in a straight vertical line, and if you would land on the riding arena on your feet if the horse were taken out from under you by magic. If you demonstrate to them the difference between popping and letting go, they may even be able to help you with this.) You may find yourself tempted to dispute this feedback and argue for your contortions – after all, they probably still feel more normal and reasonable than the weird changes you are making, and you are likely to think that you have made much bigger changes than you actually have. Remember the value of adding a camera to your feedback sessions, preferably one with a small screen so that you can view yourself in situ, and can directly compare what it feels like with what it looks like.

Remember too that all feelings are comparisons with normal, and that even the weirdest feelings become less extreme with time. You need to know whether they are becoming less extreme because you are still doing them and habituating to them well, or whether they are becoming less extreme because you have sold out on them. If they are **not** becoming less extreme, you may be doing very well right now, but there will come a time when you are well on your way to 'overkill'.

Some riders have much more pliable bodies than others. They make changes more quickly, but can reach 'overkill' so fast that they easily become confused. If your body is more fixed, you will need to drip a lot more water on the rock before you make a dent. Where do you belong on this continuum?

There is a mental component to this too. Are you the kind of person who does not really commit to learning, and who sells out on new feelings too easily? (This is probably 70 per cent of riders.) Or are you so determined to get it that you are in danger of 'overkill', even if your body is not that pliable? (This is probably about 25 per cent of riders.) The remaining 5 per cent get it just right. They are extremely good at 'reading' both their own body and the horse's response to their positioning. He becomes their guide as they search for how they can maintain 'just right' on an on-going basis.

How do you need to adjust your thinking to bring yourself closer to that 5 per cent range? You are much better off missing it by reaching 'overkill' than missing it by not going for it enough. But to 'overkill' for months on end is a waste of time. Keep getting visual feedback to help you discover exactly how much is enough.

■ *Test yourself – have you got it?*

Can you identify the seat bones and the pad in walk? At what point can you no longer maintain awareness of this? Do you lose it in other gaits? Be sure that it forms part of the checklist that you go through in walk. If you are still struggling, it may be because you are moving your backside too much in each stride. The next chapter addresses this.

■ *Off-horse exercises*

Sit on your hands, palms down, on a hard chair, and move between the extremes of rounding and hollowing your back before you point your seat bones down and settle into neutral spine. Then practise popping up, letting go, and making the pad. Firm up the pad as much as you can without losing the seat bone. You may find that you can only firm it a tiny bit before this happens. Sit like this as you drive your car. Notice if it is equally easy on both sides, or if you tend to pop up more on one than on the other, or if making the pad is easier on one side than on the other.

Chapter 3

Sitting Still in the Saddle – 'Plugging In'

■ *Description of the ideal*

The seat bone plus the pads form the rider's link with the saddle and the horse. They need to be a place of connection, so that her underside stays moulded onto the horse, and does not show any extraneous movements over and above those that match his. She is then 'plugged in'. Think of trying to put a two-pin electric plug into a socket in the dark. Instead of moving the pins backwards and forwards over the holes, they 'glunk' into place, creating a connection with the horse that goes straight into his brain, his back muscles, and his energy-circuit. It is as if he really does have 'receptors' in his back for the rider's seat bones to plug into. Her ultimate aim is to become a suction device that can draw the horse's back up under her, thus influencing his carriage. Through this way of moulding onto his back she makes a seal – and any suction device must first have a seal with the surface it is going to act on.

When the rider is correctly plugged in there is no movement in her waistband area, so instead of hollowing and/or rounding at every stride it stays very still, keeping the torso functioning as one solid block with no 'soggy' bits. The seat bones make small movements rather like walking them along (i.e. the only movement is in the hip joint) but these movements are much smaller than most riders expect them to be. Paradoxically, whilst the rider's 'insides' are moving, the outer layer of her skin appears to remain still on the saddle.

When the rider has control of the speed of her seat-bone movement, she gains control of the speed of the horse's legs. This is a vital pre-requisite for everything else.

■ *Common starting points*

Lower-tone riders with a more 'wibbly-wobbly' texture to their muscles tend to 'wibble-wobble' on the saddle, moving too much with both their backside and their waistband area. They often pride themselves on 'being supple' and 'going with the movement'; but it is much more correct to think of **leading the dance**, not following it. This means that the rider moves the horse, instead of the horse moving the rider.

The rider's 'wibbly-wobbly' communication with the horse is like a one-way 'conversation' in which she gabbles away at him without ever becoming quiet and still enough to hear his replies. Riders like this have a high 'noise-to-signal' ratio with the horse, yet they expect him somehow to know which movements are just 'noise' and which are supposed to be meaningful 'signals'.

Higher-tone riders are likely to be more in control of their seat-bone movements, but they often add a shove and push, thinking that they are 'sitting deep' and 'using their seat to drive the horse forward'. This becomes another form of 'overkill' that rarely motivates the horse, and can actually slow him down. Often this movement is done with both seat bones together and not one side at a time.

Very often, the rider at walk is not in control of the speed of the horse's legs, i.e. the tempo. The horse is then 'taking the rider' rather than the rider 'taking the horse'. This is like the difference between pushing round the pedals on a bicycle and making the wheels go round, and reaching a steep down hill and finding that you cannot pedal fast enough to keep up. At this point, you have lost control of the speed at which the wheels (which are analogous to the horse's legs) go round.

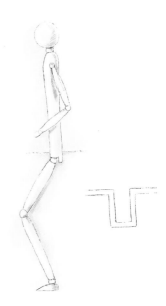

The rider who is 'plugged in' to the 'receptors' in the horse's long back muscles sits with her spine at a 90° angle to his and does not make extraneous movements that 'unplug' her.

▪ *The fix*

It is imperative that you 'take' the horse at walk before you go on into trot, and on run-away horses, the problem cannot be corrected at any other gait without first being corrected here. Be sure that your seat bones move one side at a time, not both sides together (after all, the horse does not hop like a rabbit!). Think of reducing the size of your seat-bone movements, so if they each move one inch, make it half an inch. If they move half an inch, make it one quarter of an inch, and take any shove or push out of the movement. Keep aiming to make quarter-inch movements.

Expect the horse to slow down, and think of slowing down your seat-bone movements in order to slow down the speed of his legs. If he becomes too slow, use your leg to send him forward, but realise that you must use your leg from the knee down **with nothing from the knee up changing**. Usually, when people use their leg they either shove with their backside at the same time, or it loosens to become an uncontrolled mass of wiggles. It must remain plugged in. Learning to do this is like learning to rub your stomach whilst patting your head!

Higher-tone riders who shove have the easier task. They just have to remember to stop shoving, to dare to feel as if they are doing nothing, and to risk that the horse might stop. Wobbly riders have the harder task of increasing the tone around their pelvic girdle and their waist. Think of wearing a corset that holds you more firmly, and for more help refer to Chapter 8 on narrowness.

Think of your spine as it goes down to your coccyx, and imagine that it continues down through the saddle, and about six inches down into the horse. This central axis goes along with the horse without the real and the imaginary parts of it disconnecting, and it acts like a pivot as one seat bone moves, and then the other one moves.

▪ *Troubleshooting – now*

You are likely to think that you are sitting still enough when your backside still wiggles or shoves. You are also likely to think that you do not wiggle in your waistband area when actually you do. Try moving more for a while, and then moving less. Repeat this, and use a 0 to 10 scale where 10 represents your maximum wiggle or shove, and 0 represents no wiggle or shove. How close can you get to zero?

Remember that **when you know how you wiggle, you can choose not to wiggle**. This explains why it is useful consciously, deliberately, exaggeratedly, to wiggle, so that you can learn all you can about how you do it. By learning how do you it, you concurrently discover how to **not** do it.

Have an observer validate that you really are sitting still when you think you are – and if she does not agree with you, believe her feedback and not your body! Losing the wiggles and shoves can prove tricky at first, and many people struggle with this initially. The image of your coccyx connecting down through the horse has helped many riders when all else has failed. The off-horse exercises should also help.

Realise that many riders think the horse is becoming too slow when actually he is not. Risk that he might stop, and use your leg, taking care not to unplug yourself. You cannot afford to have the leg aid take up all of your 'brain space', but must save some to monitor how your backside stays plugged in. Remind yourself to think about this before you use your leg.

▪ *Troubleshooting – on through time*

Once you have got this, you have probably got it for all time, but many riders do find it elusive at first. If you 'overkill' and stop moving your seat bones completely, your horse is likely to stop – but do not confuse this with the slowing down that will happen when you first begin to do it right. Remember that your seat bones keep moving even though your outer casing of your skin appears still.

▪ *Test yourself – have you got it?*

Become aware of the line across the back of your backside that marks where it parts company with the saddle. Throughout each phase of the horse's stride, does this line wiggle and jiggle from one bit of flesh to

Common responses

These vary from:

From low-tone riders: 'I feel as if my body is set in concrete. Surely I should be moving with him?'

From high-tone riders: 'Do you really think that I'm still shoving? It doesn't feel as if I am.'

to:

'I love it when I am in control and I am taking him rather than him taking me.'

'It's so hard to use my legs without unplugging myself.'

and:

'I couldn't bear to go back to being unplugged. There's no connection with the horse then.'

another, or is it always the same bit of flesh that stays in contact with the saddle? When you have got it, there will be no wiggles and jiggles in this line, and the same bit of flesh will always be in contact. This is a very good way to determine if you still move too much. Be strict with yourself in your assessment.

■ *Off-horse exercises*

Put your hand on your thigh, and move it backwards and forwards over the flesh. Then see how much you can move your hand whilst it stays in contact with the same bit of flesh, and moves that piece of flesh along with it. This is a good demonstration of the difference between being un-plugged, and plugged in – connected, or disconnected.

You can also put one finger on each of a friend's long back muscles, close to her spine, imagining that your fingers represent the rider's seat bones, whilst her back represents the horse's back. You can make tiny movements with your fingers, 'walking them along', and again, they can either disconnect, moving separately to the flesh and clothing beneath them, or they can move that flesh along with them and remain plugged in.

Ask a friend to lead a small horse or a pony in walk. Walk along beside the horse with your hands on his back just where your seat bones would sit, and feel how his long back muscles move under your hands. You will find that one side fills out and then the other side fills out, with no backwards-and-forwards movement. Keep this in mind as you ride, realising that you are attempting to 'plug in' to much smaller movements than most people appreciate.

Security, Strength and Power – Bear Down

■ *Description of the ideal*

The rider's primary challenge is to match the forces which the horse's movement exerts on her body; this creates an optical illusion in which she appears to sit still and do nothing. Most people think that the rider who can do this is relaxed, but actually she is stabilising herself by holding her muscles firmly.

Bearing down is the use of the abdominal muscles and forms the first stage of stabilisation. It is the same muscle use through which you clear your throat, cough, blow your nose, giggle, and defaecate, but it is maintained all the time. You naturally bear down when you sweep and push a broom away from you, but less than 5 per cent of riders use this same muscle use in riding. Good riders do it so naturally and easily that they do not know they are doing it; hence it is not delineated in the equestrian literature. (This is in some ways an enormous and unforgivable omission; but if you yourself have not been aware of the way in which you use your stomach muscles to blow your nose, it is an omission you will have to forgive. Blow your nose whilst remaining aware of your stomach, and feel what happens.)

Good riders bear down more when they need to ride the horse with more power, and they also bear down more when they need to contain or collect the horse. There is never a time when they are not bearing down.

■ *Common starting points*

Nervous riders, and riders who are determined to grow up tall, usually pull in their stomachs whilst hollowing their backs. They breathe only in the upper chest. In a scary moment they pull up and in even more, and hold their breath. Their place of strength is the shoulder girdle. They use their hand and arm to try to solve all their problems with the horse – so even though **he** may be going forwards, their stomach and hand are going backwards. This inevitably creates conflict. When the situation becomes even more scary, they resort more to their hand, and create a vicious circle whose only exit lies in bearing down and breathing well.

Less anxious but sloppy riders have their stomach muscles in neutral, not pulling in but not bearing down either. Their effect on the horse is far less positive than it could be; they will not be able to ride him powerfully, and will still resort to fixing problems with their hand.

Some riders only bear down when they need to give an aid. They do not realise the need to bear down all the time, and to increase it from this baseline when they need to be proactive.

The bottom line is that each rider has a profound existential choice: either she keeps herself in place by drawing her hand back towards her body (otherwise known as pulling), or she generates a force within her body which acts from the back towards the front. (This is otherwise known as 'staying with the horse', 'having an independent seat', 'having good hands', 'being talented' – or bearing down.) As soon as the rider is 'with' the horse in every step he takes, she becomes able to give her hand forward. As soon as she cannot match the forces which act on her body in each step, she pulls on the reins to stabilise herself, but will still probably bump towards the back of the saddle. Most riders rely on the reins to a greater or less degree. The extreme lies in 'water-skiing', where the rider puts all her weight in the stirrups and is towed along by the reins.

▪ *The fix*

Begin by making sure that you are stacked up with your seat bones pointing down, and have a straight vertical line from your pubic bone, to your belly button, sternum, and collar bone. If you tend to be hollow-backed, be sure that you are not growing tall, and that your chest aims down towards your horse's ears. Clear your throat, and then maintain that muscle use. You are now bearing down. (Your next challenge will be breathing at the same time, and this will be addressed in the next chapter.)

Your guts should push against your skin wherever there is soft tissue, i.e. all the way around your torso in the area between your ribs and hips, and in the abdominal muscles from the sternum downwards. It can be helpful to think of pulling your stomach in so that the muscles become a firm wall, and then of pushing your guts against that wall. This stops you from confusing bearing down with hanging your guts out.

Various noises make bearing down easier; clearing your throat will help you initiate it. You can then strengthen the low-down bear down at bikini-line level, by making the sound 'psst, psst'. This must have enough power to blow a blockage out of a drinking straw. The middle bear down, just below your sternum in your solar plexus can be strengthened by making the sound 'sshh, sshh'. The sound 'grrr' will strengthen everything!

Keep noticing whether or not you are bearing down as you ride. Notice too how your body responds in moments of stress, and when you want to make a downward transition. In which situations are you most tempted to pull your stomach in? Check yourself out again, and again, and again.

▪ *Troubleshooting – now*

Hollow-backed riders often read about bearing down and think, 'Oh yes, it's that thing where you push your stomach forwards.' So they hang their guts out more and subvert bearing down into a way of becoming even more hollow-backed. Even if they do not make this mistake, they are likely to not have enough 'push' into their mid-back. If you 'come to' and find that your back has hollowed, bearing down again is a two-stage process:

1. Bring your belly button and waist band back so that you are correctly stacked up.
2. Push your guts against your skin in all directions. Be sure that the push into your lower back is as strong as the push into your abdominal muscles.

Do not become confused by the apparent contradiction in the need to bring your belly button back before you are stacked up correctly enough to begin bearing down.

Round-backed riders often read about bearing down and think, 'Oh yes, it's that **down** thing,' and they pull down the front of their ribcage in a way that subverts bearing down into rounding their back more. They then sit more heavily in the saddle. They are often better off thinking of 'bear out' (around your torso, wherever there is soft tissue) rather than 'bear down'. Even if they do not make the mistake of rounding their back more, they are likely to push too much into their back, and not enough into the area beneath their sternum. This can be a place of great weakness. Strengthen it by making the sound 'sshh, sshh' as you bear down. Practise bearing down and punching yourself there, to be sure that you can keep a strong vertical wall.

Beware of your innate tendencies to round or hollow your back – they will often come back to haunt you – though you may, of course, over-correct. Either way, you need to keep ensuring that your current sense of 'right' matches reality. You **must** remain correctly stacked up as you bear down. Think of your torso like a jam jar, or tin. The contents push against the sides of the tin, but the tin must not give way or change shape. How would your torso tend to distort if you were not aware of this as a potential hazard?

Be sure that you can bear down without popping up at the same time. This can be another version of learning to rub your stomach whilst patting your head. Rest assured that it is possible with practice, even if it does not feel so right now!

Riders who are out of shape often have very little power to their bear down, and they ultimately struggle the most. If you have had babies and not worked on your abdominal strength you may have a long way to go before you get 'umph' in your bear down. Keep at it, and use the Rider's

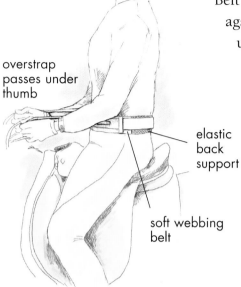

overstrap
passes under
thumb

elastic
back
support

soft webbing
belt

*The 'Rider's Belt' is worn
as low down as possible
around the pelvis. It is
elasticated and fits
tightly, creating a firm
wall that you can push
against. Pulling on the
overstrap helps you
engage the muscles of
your lower back (see
pages 66 and 67).*

Belt (see diagram) to help you create a firm wall that you can push against. If you inhabit the other end of the scale and have habitually pulled your stomach in, do not be scared of bearing down instead. You will end up with strong abdominal muscles, and a relatively flat stomach. Bearing down teaches you to draw on the strength of your core muscles. It protects your back, and if you are prone to back pain it will almost certainly help to keep you pain-free.

Many riders find bearing down so difficult that they are tempted to just ignore it whilst they improve their riding in other ways. This will only have limited success. Until you master bearing down, the lack of it will be a huge impediment to your progress.

■ *Troubleshooting – down the road*

As you strengthen your bear-down muscles and you ingrain it as a pattern, the baseline level of your bear down increases. You then increase it further when you need to become proactive. You never need to make it less because it becomes less on its own (as you forget, or as your muscles run out of steam). All you ever need to do is to make it more.

You could even spend a couple of years struggling to find enough muscle power to match the forces that the horse's movement exerts on your body. Other riders (who are themselves too sloppy) may tell you that you look stiff. Stay with the programme, and be sure that you can activate your bear-down muscles without your neck, jaw, or shoulder girdle getting in on the act. As long as this is not happening, do not let other people's comments put you off the scent.

Men are far more likely to reach 'overkill' on bearing down than women. If this ever happens, both you and your horses (especially young horses) will go into seize-up. A stronger bear down is needed as you ride the horse with more power and more collection, but a young horse is not yet ready for this.

▪ *Test yourself – have you got it?*

When you can substitute new reactions for old in a scary or difficult moment, you have got it. How do you react when the horse speeds up? When a lorry/dog/other scary item suddenly comes at you on a hack? When riding into a fence? When the horse speeds up into or after a fence? If the horse slows down or threatens to nap?

The answer to all of the above situations is **BEAR DOWN MORE**.

In what situations do you pull your stomach in, stop breathing, and resort to your hand?

What happens to your abdominal muscles in downward transitions?

Your aim is to become infallible with your bear down. In reality, you will pull your stomach in whenever you reach the edge of your 'stretch zone' and enter your 'panic zone'. It is in your 'comfort zone' that bearing down first becomes easy, but your stretch zone is where it really makes a

---

Common responses

These vary from:

'I don't believe this, surely riding shouldn't be this hard? Good riders can't possibly be doing this, they make it look so effortless!'

'I can't breathe!'

to:

'Well, I was doing it a moment ago, but I just lost it again.'

'Oh my goodness, I think I get it! I just felt myself pull my stomach in and begin pulling just as he raced off. Next time I'm going to beat him to it!'

and:

'I feel more secure and effective than I have ever been, and I'm way less panicky – as long as I remember to bear down.'

Both the tense horse and the horse who is uninterested in life and work can be likened to an unstrung bow. Whereas the horse in carriage (shown on facing page) can be thought of like a strung bow.

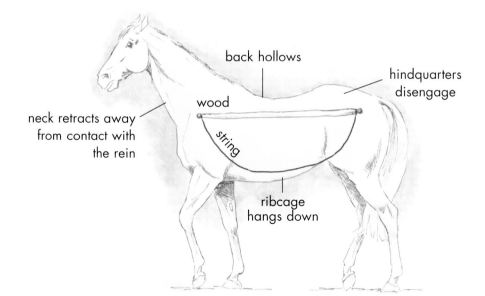

back hollows

hindquarters disengage

wood

neck retracts away from contact with the rein

string

ribcage hangs down

difference. Here, choosing new reactions over old changes your horse's response. In your panic zone you have 'lost it', and you will resort to instinctive, hand-dominant reactions. Aim to push away the boundary of each zone, so that what was your stretch zone becomes your comfort zone, and what was your panic zone becomes your stretch zone.

▪ *Off-horse exercises*

Sit on a hard chair with your seat bones pointing down, and put one hand flat on your stomach. Put the other so that your thumb and first finger are close to your spine, just above your waistband and with your fingertips resting on your long back muscles. Clear your throat and bear down. You should feel the muscles under your fingers press out against them. Realise that the horse also bears down when he works correctly, making his long back muscles bulk out just as yours do, and you will soon learn to feel this difference as you ride. The horse with a hollow back and a dangling stomach is like an unstrung bow, but bearing down shortens his stomach muscles and raises his stomach, helping him to support and lift his back so that he becomes like a strung bow. Thus there are profound parallels between

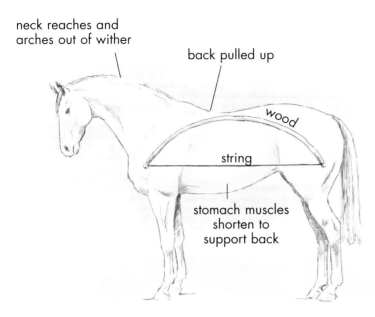

neck reaches and
arches out of wither

back pulled up

wood

string

stomach muscles
shorten to
support back

his body and yours, and you have to take on the posture and the muscle use that you want him to take on.

Bear down again with your hands resting against the sides of your waistband, and also with the fingertips of one hand low down on your bikini line. In each case, you should feel the muscles bulk out against your hand.

Practise bearing down whilst driving your car, and add noises like 'psst', 'sshh', and 'grrr' when you want more power. Practise (without the noises) in the supermarket queue, whilst making telephone calls, and if you teach riding, whilst teaching. Bear down when you are attending a job interview, asking for a raise, or negotiating for anything. You will both feel and actually **be** more powerful. If you want to become a skilful and effective rider, bearing down must become second nature, and if you do not perceive yourself as a naturally powerful person, it could profoundly change your life.

Chapter 5

Breathing – How to Bear Down and Breathe

■ *Description of the ideal*

Good riders bear down and breathe continually, without a sense of effort. The muscle use of bearing down can only be maintained indefinitely if it is accompanied by diaphragmatic breathing. This is the breathing pattern used by singers, and by people who play a wind instrument. Bearing down and breathing come so naturally to skilled riders that they fail to realise that these constitute the watershed that separates them from others who 'don't get it'.

■ *Common starting points*

Few riders breathe well, and if you find that you run out of breath after riding a few circles in the school, it is bound to be your breathing technique that limits you, and not your overall fitness. Even if you are not aware of your breathing as a limitation, notice how far down your torso you inflate with each in-breath. Some riders barely reach their sternum, others find that the breath goes down to their belly button. Few find that it reaches to their bikini line.

When riders hold their breath, they do so after a short in-breath that is almost a gasp. The breath, their chest and their shoulders go up, inflating only their upper chest. They then forget to breathe out.

Dressage judges often report that riders do their best work riding down the centre line at the end of a test. This is the point at which they think 'Phew!' breathe out, and finally allow themselves to settle.

■ *The fix*

When you are riding, the breath must go **down** (not up into your upper chest) and reach all the way down to your bikini line. It is helpful to think of a chemistry flask shape inside you, with a long neck that passes down your windpipe, and extends even lower so that the bowl rests in your pelvis. As you breathe in, the air must go all the way down the long neck into the round bowl. It also helps to think of a pair of bellows that sucks air in. It helps to think of feeling the coldness of the air as it passes down the front of your windpipe. (In my experience, you can make this idea work even on hot days!) If you feel that the air gets stuck on its passage down, think of breathing in some 'block dissolver' along with it. Make friends with the block; talk to it nicely, ask it to let go, and be quietly persistent, taking the time it takes to find a way through it.

On the out-breath, the bowl in your pelvis must initially stay inflated. Imagine a tap on your midline at bikini-line level, and pretend that the air leaves your body through that tap. Make the sound 'phsst!' as you breathe out. This will keep your guts pressing out against your skin (i.e. it will keep you bearing down) on the out-breath. As you run out of air, your torso will inevitably deflate, allowing it to inflate on the next in-breath.

Realise that it is cultural insanity to tell our horses (and ourselves) to 'breathe in' as we tighten girths and belts. This only makes sense in military-type breathing, where you breathe in whilst inflating your chest, sucking in your stomach, and

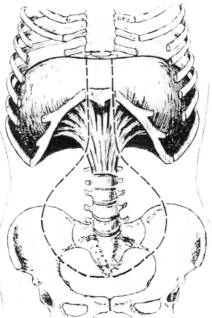

The ribcage has been cut away to expose the diaphragm and the imaginary conical flask in the abdominal cavity.

standing to attention. In good breathing, your ribcage, waist and abdomen **inflate** as you breathe in.

■ *Troubleshooting – now*

Which is harder, bearing down whilst breathing in, or bearing down whilst breathing out?

If the problem is breathing in, think about the chemistry flask analogy and refer also to the off-horse exercise below. If the problem is breathing out, think of the tap at bikini-line level, and make the sound 'phsst!' on each out-breath. Don't be shy about this, it is a tremendous help!

It will be harder to breathe if you are bearing down to your maximum (i.e. on 10 out of 10). Identify your 10 out of 10 level by clearing your throat and creating your strongest bear down. You may need to back off to 6 out of 10 to be able to bear down and breathe.

■ *Troubleshooting – on through time*

Once you have got this, you have got it for all time, apart from the odd scary moment that might still catch you out. But changing your breathing pattern is not easy, and it requires great dedication and commitment. (What is more 'you' than how you breathe?) Realise that you will not breathe one way for twenty-three hours a day, and then breathe another way on the twenty-fourth hour when you are riding your horse. You have to change how to breathe, period, so practise when driving your car and in everyday situations. Once you have managed to bear down and breathe for a three-hour stretch, you will be well over the worst, and will probably transfer your new skill into your riding with relative ease. There are significant life advantages to breathing well: your resting heart rate and respiration rates will drop, as you will be using your lung capacity to maximum advantage. Do not give up. If you breathe well, you may even live longer!

> ## Common responses
>
> These vary from:
>
> 'You're trying to tell me that people do this naturally? It takes some believing.'
>
> 'I can only bear down if I hold my breath, I can't do it and breathe at the same time.'
>
> to:
>
> 'It's getting much easier, and it makes a huge difference. But I still occasionally catch myself sucking my stomach in and barely breathing.'

■ *Test yourself – have you got it?*

When you are riding in walk, count the movement of the horse's forelegs, looking at his shoulders if you need to. As you count left, right, left, right (i.e. the four counts that constitute two full strides), you breathe in. On the next four counts breathe out. Then see if you can make each in-breath and out-breath last for six counts. If you cannot do this, your breathing is still restricted.

At rising trot. you should be able to make an in-breath last for three sits, and the out-breath last for three sits. If you can only do two, your lung capacity is still limited. This follows through to sitting trot.

In canter, you should be able to make each in-breath and out-breath last for at least four strides.

What happens in scary moments? Remind yourself to bear down and breathe whenever you approach a spooky place. Pay particular attention to breathing out: remember that the rider who holds her breath takes a short, sharp, 'up' in-breath, and then forgets to breathe out. Make the sound 'phsst!' to help you bear down, breathe down, and breathe out through the spook. Realise that your horse probably knows more about how you are breathing than you do, and that he will take his cue from you. The last horse you want to be riding in this situation is one who is holding his breath!

You have only really got this when it is natural, easy, and how you breathe in your everyday life. Keep at it, and one day you will marvel that you ever had the problem.

◾ *Off-horse exercises*

Put the palms of your hand on the back, lower part of your ribcage. Your little fingers are to the top, your thumbs to the bottom. Imagine that air enters your body along the top edge of your hand, as if you had gills like a fish. Feel your back expand under your hands as you breathe in, and be sure that all the activity of breathing happens from this level down, i.e. not higher in your back or in your upper chest. Realise that breathing well involves your back much more than your front. Using this technique you will find yourself bearing down as you breathe in, even if you do not make a conscious decision to do so.

As you breathe out, place the fingertips of one hand on your midline at bikini-line level. Make the sound 'phsst!', and feel your guts push against your fingers. As you breathe in again, move your hands to your back, and feel your back expand beneath them. This time, breathe out thinking of the tap at bikini-line level, but keeping your hands on your back. You should feel your back push **even more firmly** against your hands. This is very important. As the out-breath progresses that push will decrease as you inevitably deflate. This prepares you to inflate as you breathe in again.

If you find yourself struggling and getting nowhere, consider booking a lesson with a singing or voice teacher. Tell her that you want to breathe rather than sing! You might also consider seeing a bodyworker. The 'block' may be that your diaphragm is in spasm (as it often is in fearful people) and you will not be able to release this on your own.

Practise bearing down and breathing whilst you drive your car, and in all sorts of everyday situations. Practise, practise, practise. Despite the difficulty you feel now, it can become natural and easy.

Chapter 6

Firming up the Body –
Muscle Tone, and the
Learning Process

▪ *Description of the ideal*

Muscle tone, of which bearing down is an example, constitutes the hidden dimension of riding. Tone refers to the texture of the muscles.

Skilled riders have the high tone that gives the body a texture like putty, and this keeps it firm and stable. Paradoxically, the high-tone rider looks as if she is doing nothing and is conventionally thought of as 'relaxed'. Lower tone gives the body a texture more like jelly, and leaves the rider much more 'flopsy', wobbly and uncoordinated. To understand this, think of the difference between a rag doll, which 'gives' anywhere, and a wooden puppet, with metal rings forming the joints of the ankle, knee and hip, wrist, elbow and shoulder. Like the ideal rider, this puppet is stable between the joints, but 'gives' at the joints.

Having 'rag doll' texture causes the rider to rely on her hands to stabilise herself (using the pull from front to back that was discussed in Chapter 4). Observers then see the tension in her hand, arm and shoulder girdle and regard her as stiff, even though this tension is a compensation for the **lack** of tone elsewhere in her body.

■ *Common starting points*

Men naturally have 35 per cent higher muscle tone than women, and this is one of their biggest advantages as riders. Tone gives a firmness to the body that the vast majority of women struggle to find. Think of the rider like a stuffed toy – higher-tone riders (and horses) are like brand new stuffed toys, whilst lower-tone riders (and horses) have far less 'stuffing', like elderly stuffed toys that have seen better days.

Less talented riders have less stuffing throughout their body, and virtually everyone has weak places that show up to the trained eye.

Women often do not have enough tone around the pelvic girdle. (See also Chapter 8, on narrowness, which describes more ways of working with this.) Their lack of tone stops them from getting enough of a push from the back towards the front. It also contributes to the 'spongy buttock syndrome', in which the rider's skin remains in contact with the saddle in sitting trot, but the flesh between her seat bones and the saddle squashes down and then expands just like a sponge. This never happens to men, whose flesh stays 'squashed' down, keeping their seat bones down on the saddle.

Sometimes, the pelvis and upper body are well toned, but there is an area of 'shifting sand' around the waist, where the rider experiences involuntary movement that she cannot easily control.

Many riders 'run out of stuffing' in their lower legs, and find that these wave about, especially in sitting trot. Often, one side of the torso is less stuffed, contributing to a collapsed hip in which the rider's spine goes off axis. One thigh and calf are usually less toned than the other, compounding the asymmetry and steering issues. The forces that act on the rider's body, especially whilst riding on a circle, make these differences more obvious, and they are a significant part of the 'grist to the mill' in learning to ride well. In lateral work their effects are magnified.

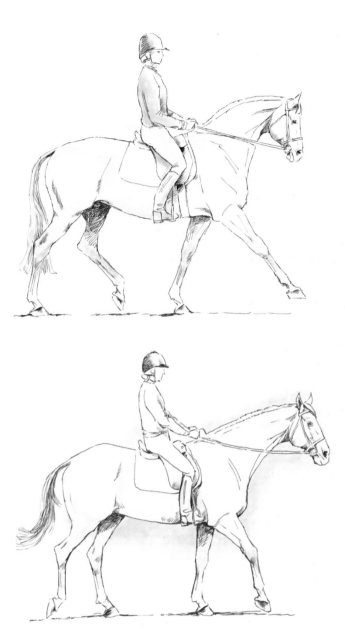

When rider and horse have high muscle tone they are like brand new stuffed toys, almost 'bursting out of their skin'.

Same horse and rider 'unstuffed'.

■ *The fix*

The fix begins with bearing down and plugging in. Both of these firm up the pelvic area and help the rider to get control of her seat-bone movement. To increase the tone in the sacrum area, think of wearing a corset that laces up across your back, pulling both sides in towards the middle. If you have trouble making this image work for you, a Rider's Belt can help (see page 38). Then think of beginning your bear down in your back. Imagine that you are a sandwich-board man, and that the back sandwich board is pushed up towards the front sandwich board as if you had no thickness. Then, your guts push against your skin, and you aim that push towards the horse's neck, thinking of pushing it out and away from you.

If the tone in your pelvic area is weak, it can also help to think of 'tying your washing up tighter'. If you could take all your dirty washing and tie it into a bundle using an old sheet, that bundle would represent your pelvis. As you 'tie the bundle tighter' it is as if you shrink your pelvis and hold it firmer. Imagine that you could shrink it to a point, which is your centre of gravity. You must ride that point, always being in control of it, so that it does not wobble around.

To firm up the thighs, think of your thigh bones like iron bars. Is one firmer, and one more mushy and soggy? If you divide each thigh bone into

---

Common responses

These vary from:

'Why does it have to be this hard? It's just not fair, good riders make it look so easy!'

'I'll never learn to keep my legs still, and I don't believe that my spongy butt will ever go away.'

to:

'You're right, enjoying the journey is really what it's about. But I've always just wanted to arrive.'

and:

'I get such a kick out of discovering how this works and becoming more skilful.'

---

thirds (up near the pelvis, in the middle, and down by your knee), which thirds are firmest and which are soggiest on each leg? Think of the firmness of the bone extending inch by inch from the stronger areas into the areas of weakness. Your bones ideally form a framework around the horse, as if you are a container and he is a liquid, so a soggy framework can lead to all sorts of distortions.

Firming up calves that are low tone and wobbly is more difficult, and this is addressed in Chapter 10, particularly pages 89 and 90.

■ *Troubleshooting – now*

The primary issue at this stage is to change your concept of riding skills, and what it takes to learn them. You need to take on board the idea that riding well is about developing the muscle tone that enables you to stabilise your body (whilst keeping your joints free to move). Realise that this is a long-term learning process that will concurrently challenge and develop your understanding of the rider/horse interaction. Many of the early barriers to this are inside your head, and originate in the fact that the horse world has sold you a different concept of riding skills, of learning, and of how the rider does (or does not) affect the horse. Added to this, most people want the learning process to be different to, and easier than, it actually is. Begin by diagnosing your low-tone areas, with help if necessary, realising that as you gradually learn how to fix them, so riding will slowly reveal its secrets to you.

■ *Troubleshooting – on through time*

As you learn, the process involves fixing the weak spots that are currently most significant, and realising as you do so just how they were limiting your own and your horse's performance. Then, just as you are feeling euphoric about the changes created by your discovery, so your horse will find the next loophole and reveal to you the next weakest area that you need to work on. Fix this one, pass through the euphoric stage, and then face disappointment as your horse shows you the next most important flaw in your technique. So it goes on. The trick is not to allow euphoria to get the better of you, for this will always be followed by the tragic disappointment of discovering that you have not 'got it' as a *fait accompli*, but have only 'got' a small piece in the puzzle. Remember, journeying is not half the fun, it's all there is. There is no such thing as arriving.

As you journey, align yourself well, bear down, plug in, and learn to breathe well. As you watch really good riders, realise that their stillness, power and influence comes from bearing down, and having high tone. Do not buy into the myth that you can emulate them by relaxing.

■ *Test yourself – have you got it?*

Are you becoming more secure and stable in your riding? Are you aligning yourself well and sitting more still? Are you actively 'dripping water on the rock', clocking up the repetitions that your nervous system needs in order to ingrain these new patterns? Do you have a checklist of reminders to use when you are riding? **Do** you remind yourself? How often? This is a new way to engage your brain, and it is probably very different to the way you are used to thinking. But it is the only one that works.

When you can have a big breakthrough and not be overtaken by euphoria, you have got it. Euphoria is a sign that your performance and your identity are tied in together, i.e. if you ride well, you become a good rider and by implication a good or better person. Conversely, if you ride badly you become a bad rider and by implication a bad or worse person. This means that every ride – and even every transition or every circle – has the power to prove that you are a good or bad person. This puts your horse under huge stress, for your self-image is determined by the way he goes. This means that you will resort to all sorts of dubious tactics to make sure that he goes 'right'.

When your horse can stick his nose up in the air and you do not immediately try to pull or 'fiddle' it down, you have got it, for you have not bought into the cultural ethos that this makes you a bad rider. You have separated your performance from your identity when, instead of pulling your horse's head down, you can live with the fact that this happened, you can be seen as an imperfect rider, and take the time it takes fix the situation by bringing his back up again. You have then realised that a rosebud is no less worthy than a rose – it simply exists at a different stage of development. This enables you to learn riding skills with far less emotional angst.

When you realise that you are a good person, and that riding skills are just a set of learned behaviours, you have got it. The lack of these skills then simply means that there is more learning to go through.

■ *Off-horse exercises*

In learning about stabilisation and muscle tone a physioball is a huge help, since it mirrors the biomechanical challenges of riding. Riders up to 5ft 6ins need a 65cm diameter ball, taller riders need a 75cm ball. The ball needs to be blown up firmly, and this could take several attempts as a new ball will expand beyond the point where it appeared firm. It will then need occasional top-ups.

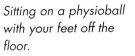

Sitting on a physioball with your feet off the floor.

Begin by sitting on the ball with your legs in an 'on-horse' position. You might want to put the ball in a doorway so that you can steady yourself by putting your hands on the door jambs. Or you may want to place it near to a sturdy table that you can grab for support. Then take your feet off the floor and balance on the ball. You will find that this is easier said than done – and you may become grateful that your horse has a leg at each corner and does not overtly lose his balance when you do! Practise, and you will find that your body soon learns from its mistakes, and that your tendencies to overcorrect become smaller until you can begin to home in on the balance point.

Learn to balance on the ball with your hands on the tops of your thighs as shown. In the process, notice how you tend to fall off the ball. Are you having trouble on the back/front plane, suggesting that you still tend to either round or hollow your back, or are your difficulties on the side/side plane? Notice which way your shoulders go off axis. You will tend to fall off axis in the same way when you ride.

Put your feet on the floor, again in an 'on-horse' position. Beginning

(a) The beginning position to get into the prone bridge, and (b) rolling out into this position, (c) holding it, and (d) marching in it.

From sitting on the ball, roll like this (a) into the supine bridge; (b) holding the supine bridge; and (c) marching in this position. to maintain neutral spine, think of keeping your hips and your 'withers' (i.e. thoracic curve of your spine) up.

cautiously, have a partner attempt to push and pull the ball out from under you, in all sorts of directions. Your job is to stabilise yourself and the ball. Then have her push on your shoulders, your back, your upper chest or your sides, realising that this must be done carefully, slowly building up each push, and not resorting to surprise, speed, or a competitive attitude. Which pushes make it hardest for you to stabilise yourself? What do you have to do to stay stable?

The illustrations opposite show exercises to develop strength in the back muscles and the abdominal muscles respectively. When you reach the stages of lifting each leg, go carefully – it is much harder than it looks. Your aim is to keep your torso horizontal throughout, and not to lift, drop or twist your pelvis.

The following exercise also develops strength in the back muscles and in bearing down. Ideally use a large bath towel, putting it around your back under your armpits, so that you can hold onto it with your hands. You can also use a rolled-up sweatshirt, or any long-sleeved jacket that will not stretch. Stand in an 'on-horse' position, making sure that your seat bones point down, and that you are not leaning back, hollowing your back, etc. If you stand sideways-on to a large mirror, you can check this visually.

Make sure that your shoulders and elbows are pulled down throughout the exercise. Then push back against the bath towel at the same time as you pull on it, being sure that your alignment does not change. Do this for at least thirty seconds before you move it down about four inches, and repeat the process. Keep repeating it until the bath towel is around your sacrum, lying in the same place as the Rider's Belt (see the illustration on page 38). It then performs the same function as the belt. As you do the exercise, notice if you are bearing down. I think you will find that it 'just happens' as your back muscles engage strongly. You now understand the concept of strength in riding terms, and what good riders mean when they say that they are 'doing nothing'!

The 'marching' exercise in Chapter 9, and the 'dead leg' exercise and the challenges in Chapter 10, also concern muscle tone and stabilisation, and you may want to look at them now for a more complete understanding of the topic.

Chapter 7

Sitting Lightly – Supporting Your Own Bodyweight

■ *Description of the ideal*

Good riders sit as if they were on one of those stools that are good for your posture, where you sit on a slope and rest your shins on a slope. This means that virtually the whole area of suede on a pair of suede-seated breeches is weight-bearing. By spreading the weight-bearing surface down the thigh (and therefore forward on the horse's ribcage) the rider avoids placing all her weight in the middle of the horse's back where he can hollow it away from her. Her thigh acts like a lever, and the weight acting down at her knee counterbalances the weight of her upper body. The thigh muscles experience stresses similar to those of standing in an on-horse position. Their eccentric contraction serves to support the rider's bodyweight, making her less of a burden for the horse to carry. This muscle use is so powerful that it enables the rider to become a suction device that can draw the horse's back up under her instead of squashing it down.

To understand how high muscle tone supports your bodyweight, think of picking up a child who does not want to be moved. She relaxes completely and makes herself into dead weight, as does the proverbial 'sack of potatoes' rider, whose heaviness squashes the horse's back down. The child (and the rider) who **wants** to be picked up positively aids the process by keeping her muscle tone high. Her apparent lightness, along with the leverage of the rider's thigh, can change the horse's carriage from that of the unstrung bow shown on page 40, to that of the strung bow shown on page 41. Instead of the horse's back being hollow with his stomach hanging down, his stomach muscles shorten and his back is drawn up, creating the beautiful carriage and movement of the dressage horse.

Good riders virtually hang the horse, the saddle, the underside of their thigh and their lower leg from their thigh bone and the muscles along the top of the thigh. This is not the same as relaxing!

■ *Common starting points*

Many riders sit too heavily, treating the horse like an armchair, and surrendering their bodyweight to him – see illustration right. Some virtually grind their seat bones down into his back. Riders who think of 'sitting deep', 'using the seat' and 'driving the horse forward' are likely to make this mistake. The more weight a rider has on her backside, the less she spreads her weight down through her thighs. If she also tucks her backside underneath her, her knees will come more up and away from the saddle with her thighs rotating outwards. The more this happens, the more her horse will hollow his back. Also, sitting heavily tends to **deaden** the horse, making him less willing to go forward and less 'pingy' in his gaits. It is as if he were a trampoline, whose innate bounce can be enhanced or deadened by the tonal quality and the weightedness of the rider's body.

In contrast, very nervous riders are often found perched up off the horse's back, barely sitting at all. They tend to sit on their fork and lean forwards, and to be hollow-backed, with their seat bones pointing backwards – see illustration right. These are the riders who grip with their knees, and

Left: Round-backed rider, in armchair seat.

Below: Hollow-backed rider, perched on saddle.

'Sophisticated' hollow-backed rider.

Well-aligned rider.

who have given this idea such bad press. Whilst they may be supporting their own bodyweight, they are 'pinged' up off their horses rather too easily!

Would-be dressage riders who ride with an almost vertical thigh also do not support any of their bodyweight more forward on the horse's ribcage. Again, the thigh cannot act as a lever; all of their weight is down in the hollow of the horse's back, which I call the 'man-trap'. This posture predisposes him to hollow his back even more. The rider too will have a hollow back, as it is impossible to make the thigh vertical without the waistband coming forward – see illustration left.

▪ *The fix*

The rider must set her stirrups so that the thigh bone lies at 45° to the ground, with the thigh muscles rotated around to the back of it, and the whole of the inner thigh resting snugly against the saddle. (See drawing below left.) It is easy to understand how the armchair seat and the vertical thigh put all of the rider's weight down into the hollow of the horse's back. It is less easy to understand how using the thigh as a lever actually enables the rider to create suction, and to draw the horse's back up under her – but simply by virtue of not squashing it down, you begin to draw it up. This effect is made far more powerful by using the 'front tendons' as described in the dismounted exercise below.

Keep thinking of the posture stool, and of supporting your own bodyweight. Imagine that you are sitting on a big balloon, and that you do not want to burst it. In fact, you want to think of it filling up with air underneath you, for the horse's back will become higher and wider as he comes into carriage. Throughout this process, you should be able to feel the tendons at the corners of your pubic bone resting on the saddle. It is common for these, and the top inner thighs to get quite sore when you are riding. Take this as a sign that you are doing well. If you cannot activate these muscles, place the back of your hand against the saddle under the top inside of your thigh, and squash it.

The bony knobble in the inside of your knee should also rest on the saddle (unless the saddle really does not fit you and/or is badly designed). Imagine a hook on each one, and hook them onto an imaginary iron bar that passes through the horse's ribcage. Realise that this bar is not elastic, so it does not pull your knees in together, it just keeps them in place. Have a friend try to pull your knee off the saddle. She should not be able to do so.

■ *Troubleshooting – now*

Be sure that the whole length of your inside thigh is lying against the saddle. Even though you have read my words, you are unlikely to put your thighs on the saddle firmly enough. This idea shocks many people who have been told that they must relax their thighs and take their knees off the saddle, but **the thigh can only be weight-bearing if it is against the saddle**. Good riders who do this well will tell you that their thigh is relaxed, but if you tried to slide your fingers between their thigh and the saddle, I guarantee that they would not fit!

Do not allow your knees to make a firmer contact with the saddle than the top inside of your thighs. Think of the thighs contacting the saddle by making a narrower 'V' shape around the horse, i.e. they must narrow in at the top as well as at the knee.

When you think of sitting lightly and of activating your front tendons (see the dismounted exercise below), do not pop up by tensing the muscles between your seat bones and the saddle. It is the top and the inside of your thigh that becomes active as you support your bodyweight, not the muscles under your backside. You must sit on the saddle, and not become light by 'un-sitting' yourself (as in the two-point seat, or the posture of a nervous novice). Realise that you cannot become a suction device unless you are making contact with the surface you are acting on.

Be sure as well that you do not grow tall as you think of sitting light. People hear this idea and become tempted to pull their ribs up away from their hips, thinking that this makes them lighter. It is a big mistake. You must concurrently keep your seat bones pointing down, and the hollow out of your back. Stay short, with your ribs dropping down towards your

Most riders stretch up from the waist and stretch down from the waist as in (a). In doing this, they hollow their backs and push down into the stirrups. In learning how to counteract this tendency, they have to feel as if they are doing the opposite, bringing both halves of their body in towards the middle, as in (b). When they establish correct carriage from the horse, they go through a sequence: initially they drop down, bringing their ribs towards their hips and resting their foot in the stirrup. Then they think of the horse coming up underneath them, and bringing them up, as in (c). It is this sense of coming up that good riders talk about.

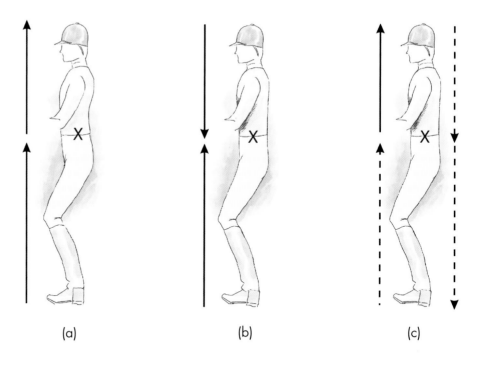

(a)   (b)   (c)

hips; but from underneath you, think of the horse coming up.

This is a paradox that your brain and body have (sooner or later) to understand and embody. Supporting your own bodyweight and sitting lightly are difficult ideas to explain and understand on paper, and there are many potential misinterpretations. A friend has to see you taking on the form of the riders in the drawings on pages 14 and 49 (top).

■ *Troubleshooting – on through time*

Once you know how to use your thigh muscles, you have probably got it for all time, even though there are important refinements to add later. You are more likely to make the mistake of losing the correct stack-up of your upper body, and if your old habit is strongly ingrained you will revert to it. Alternatively, you will home in on the ideal of neutral spine by alternating between too round a back and too hollow a back, and whenever you round your back, your thighs will tend to rotate outwards, away from the saddle.

However well you ride, it never hurts to reach around the back of your

> ## Common responses
>
> These vary from:
>
> 'But I feel as if I am gripping. Surely this can't be right?'
>
> 'How can I keep my ribs down and keep bearing down without becoming heavy? It seems like a contradiction.'
>
> 'Thinking of sitting light makes me want to pop up and grow tall.'
>
> to:
>
> 'Oh, that really makes a difference. If I can just keep supporting myself with my thighs then think about suction I can feel his back come up.'
>
> and:
>
> 'That difficult young horse I rode yesterday really made my inner thighs sore, which is amazing because I rarely experience that any more. The amount I do on "auto-pilot" is enough for most horses, but it's not enough on that youngster.'

thigh, grab some of the flesh that is currently against the saddle, and pull it away from the saddle so that it becomes part of the back of your thigh.

■ *Test yourself – have you got it?*

If you are really working hard to support your own bodyweight and not to fall back down the horse's man-trap, it can feel as if someone could slide a piece of paper between you and the saddle, even though you are still in contact with it. How much are you relying on the horse to hold you up, and how much are you holding yourself (and therefore potentially his back) up?

■ *Off-horse exercises*

Stand in an 'on-horse' position. If you stay there for a while the muscles along the top of the thigh start to ache. This is because your thigh acts as a lever. When you are riding and you have your inner thighs on the saddle, those muscles can also take some of that strain (and ultimately, though not at this stage, so can the outer thigh muscles).

Sit on a firm chair with your calves vertical. Place the fingers of one hand in the angle between one thigh and your torso, and lift your knee. Feel for two strong tendons, which will stick up like taut pieces of rope (if you do not dig your fingers in hard enough to separate them, you may only feel one). Then, put your opposite hand on your knee, and hold it down as you attempt to lift it. Again, the tendons should stick up. Notice how your thigh muscles change shape. Hold your front tendons up as you ride, but be sure that you do not pop up at the same time.

To better understand how your thighs act as a lever, kneel with your backside resting on your heels, and place a pad under your knees. Put one hand just below your sternum, and the other at the same height on your back. Slowly raise your backside until it is above your knees, and then lower it again. Do not lift your chin and your chest as you kneel up. Your hands are there to remind you that your front must stay short, and your

Kneeling up and down. From starting position (a) you can either lengthen your front, as in (b), which hollows your back and takes all the strain off your thighs, or you can lever yourself up from your thighs, as in (c). There is then no change in your torso, but considerable muscle work is done by your thighs.

back must not hollow. Your thighs will soon tell you if you are performing the exercise correctly, and if they do not begin to hurt very soon you can safely presume that you are pulling yourself up from your stomach muscles instead of levering yourself up from your thigh muscles. For an additional challenge, pause on the way up and the way down.

As you strengthen your quadriceps muscles you also need to keep stretching them. My earlier book, *For the Good of the Rider,* includes a range of useful stretches.

Buy yourself a 'Thighmaster' or, better still, a 'Pilates Fitness Circle' (see Resources, page 134). Both devices create a resistance that you can push your inner thighs against. You need to become strong here, but you also need to balance this strength by doing adductor stretches.

Chapter 8

Using the Back –
Narrowness (The 'Pinch')

■ *Description of the ideal*

Good riders use the muscles of the lower back in a way that draws both sides of their pelvis towards their midline, making them narrower. It is as if they make a narrower 'V' shape, where the 'V' extends from their back into each thigh. As the back narrows, the thighs and knees do not come off the saddle, making the 'V' wider. Initially this is instinctive to most riders. The increased muscle tone generated by this narrowness enables the rider to firm up her pelvic girdle, to plug in, to begin to bear down in her back, and to support her own bodyweight more effectively. It ties these concepts in together, and makes them all easier.

This narrowness also increases the rider's ability to steer and position the horse. It is as if her body becomes an 'A' frame around him, which contains him within it. Most riders have an 'A' frame that is much too wide, allowing the horse enough leeway to bulge and wobble within it; they then try to correct these deviations with their hands and legs. Sophisticated steering uses the rider's 'A' frame and her thighs to steer the horse's wither, and good riders do not fall into the trap of trying to steer his nose with their reins. (This may bring his nose to the inside of a turn or circle, but his wither will go to the outside, and the horse will follow his wither, falling out on the circle.) Even more skilled riders have learned to become so narrow that their pelvis fits across each of the horse's long back muscles in the ideal way. This is a precise and sophisticated concept that enables the rider to steer the horse even more effectively.

▪ *Common starting points*

The vast majority of riders are too wide. People who have 'wideness' ingrained as a significant pattern tend to trudge as they walk. They lack a spring in their step, since the muscles and ligaments that 'narrow' the pelvis help to create this spring. The most wide riders have the greatest difficulty with pelvic muscle tone and plugging in. They tend to be heavy, 'down' riders, and since they are falling off the sides of the horse they cannot 'get hold of' his ribcage with their pelvis and thighs. This leaves their hands and legs as the only tools that they have left to ride with. This is destabilising and ineffective.

Some riders, especially jumping riders, have their knees so tightly against the saddle that they do not create an 'A' frame around him. Their thighs either form parallel lines, or a 'V' with its point in front of the horse's chest. As a result, they tend to ping up and off the horse like a clothes peg.

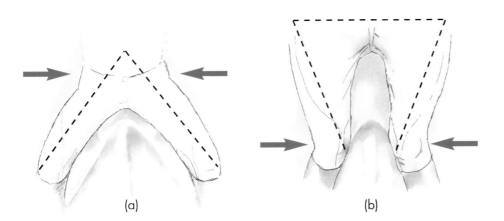

(a)   (b)

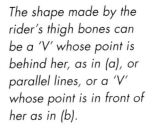

The shape made by the rider's thigh bones can be a 'V' whose point is behind her, as in (a), or parallel lines, or a 'V' whose point is in front of her as in (b).

■ *The fix*

Imagine that you are wearing some kind of corset around your pelvis that has laces across the back. As the corset is laced up, the two sides of you are drawn in towards your centre line. Visualise the deeper layer of muscles shown opposite drawing the two sides of you towards the middle. Try to make sense out of this idea at walk; it will not make sense at halt, and will be hard to do in trot until you have sensed it at walk. It could make plugging in much easier, for without enough tone across your back you cannot control the wobbles that unplug you.

When you feel narrower, think of your bear down beginning in your back. Think of pushing the back of you towards the front of you as if you have no thickness. Remember the image of the sandwich-board man from Chapter 6, page 50. Then you pull your stomach in, think of the muscles like a wall, push against that wall, and aim the push down the corridor made by your lower arms and the reins, with the aim of pushing the horse's head and neck away from you. If his back is hollow and his ears near your chin, it is as if he is pushing back at you – as if someone had put her hand on his muzzle and forced it backwards (as you see in the horse on page 40). This pushes his muzzle back into his poll, his poll back into his neck, his neck back into his wither, and his wither back into his back, forming the hollow of the 'man-trap' that you have almost certainly fallen back into.

Beginning your bear down in your back literally doubles its power, helping you to create a push forward which is stronger than the horse's push back. But these lower back muscles are very low tone and 'sleepy' in most people, so you may find it difficult to activate them. Imagine that someone has placed their hand on your lower back, and pushed your back towards your front. Keeping thinking of this and of 'lacing up' until your brain eventually manages to 'talk to' these muscles.

Think of your thigh bones, and imagine that they could extend (by magic) in front of your knees and back behind you. Do they form parallel lines, are they a 'V' shape whose point lies behind you, or a 'V' shape whose point lies in front of the horse's chest? (Logically this latter option sounds impossible, but riders who 'pinch with their knees' concurrently splay

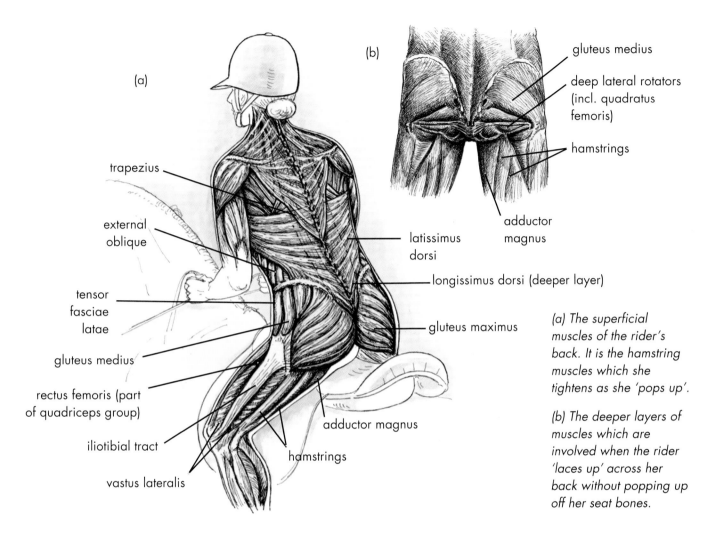

(a)

(b)

trapezius

external
oblique

tensor
fasciae
latae

gluteus medius

rectus femoris (part
of quadriceps group)

iliotibial tract

vastus lateralis

hamstrings

adductor magnus

latissimus
dorsi

longissimus dorsi (deeper layer)

gluteus maximus

gluteus medius

deep lateral rotators
(incl. quadratus
femoris)

hamstrings

adductor
magnus

*(a) The superficial
muscles of the rider's
back. It is the hamstring
muscles which she
tightens as she 'pops up'.*

*(b) The deeper layers of
muscles which are
involved when the rider
'laces up' across her
back without popping up
off her seat bones.*

apart across their back, and can feel as if their thighs create a 'V' which is this way round.) You need to get the point back behind you, and if you have to make a 'V' out of parallel thighs, be careful that you do not widen the 'V' down by your knees as you narrow your back. Think of being narrow across your back, narrow between your seat bones (as if you are holding the horse's spine in between them), narrow between the tendons at the top inside of your thighs, and narrow down the whole length of your thighs.

How far back behind you is the point of the 'V'? Is it behind the horse's tail, over his croup, or closer to the saddle? How high is the point of the 'V'? The more you are thinking of your thighs being out in front of you

Common responses

These vary from:

'I just don't get it. I can't seem to feel those muscles in my back at all.'

'I keep taking my knees off the saddle every time I think of narrowing in.'

'Every time I narrow in I pop up… this is going to take forever.'

to:

'This explains why everything else has been so difficult.'

and:

'I feel way firmer, lighter and more effective when I get it. There is far more power in my bear down.'

'It makes so much difference. And thinking of steering the horse's wither between the "V" shape of my thighs is a revelation. It makes me so much less tempted to pull on the inside rein.'

rather than vertical, the lower the point will be.

You want to get the point of the 'V' to be about three inches behind the back of the saddle, at half the height of your sacrum. Keep working on this until you have the point this low down and have become this narrow. The change you need to make will inevitably happen in stages. Do not give up until you have reached this ideal.

If you can make no sense at all of this concept, try riding with the Rider's Belt (see page 38) and using the over-strap. You should find that it teaches you how to 'switch on' the muscles across your lower back. You may even find that you are sore in them the next day. This is a good sign.

▪ *Troubleshooting – now*

The biggest danger is taking your thigh and knee off the saddle as you narrow across your back. The whole length of the 'V' must become narrower. The other danger is popping up as you narrow in (see Chapter 2, on seat bones, page 23). Many riders have difficulty separating their narrowing-in muscles (which lie across their lower back) from their popping-up muscles (which lie under their backside). Again, this is like learning how to rub your stomach and pat your head. Remember that you do not want so much muscle between your seat bones and the saddle that you cannot feel your seat bones. The ideal is to have a muscle pad to the outside of each seat bone, thus widening your base of support, but not to have the muscle tighten so much that the pad moves in under the seat bone (see page 24).

About 10 per cent of riders find narrowness really difficult – but they are the ones who have the most to gain by becoming narrow. Do not give up until you can sense that the point of the 'V' is a few inches behind the saddle, and half the height of your sacrum. If you have trouble beginning your bear down in your back, suspect that you still need to narrow in more.

▪ *Troubleshooting – on through time*

The benefits of this are so great that once you have got the idea, you will be highly motivated to keep doing it. It is impossible to become too narrow across your back: in fact, this is an idea that good riders have developed further, taking the concept of narrowness all the way up their torso.

▪ *Test yourself – have you got it?*

Can you plug in? Begin your bear down in your back? Support your own bodyweight? Narrowness is implicated in all of these, and if you are still struggling, suspect that this might be the difference that makes the difference.

Does the point of your 'V' lie at the correct point? Another big test lies in the ease with which you can steer the horse's wither.

■ *Off-horse exercises*

Stand in an 'on-horse' position, and think of aiming your left seat bone diagonally towards the bony knobble on the inside of your right ankle, and your right seat bone diagonally towards the knobble on the inside of your left ankle. Then, think of pushing your thighs and heels outwards, as if against a resistance. Be careful not to roll onto the outer edge of your foot; instead, be sure that your heels push out only in a way that makes your toes point in. Riders who also ski have likened this to doing a snow plough, but with your skis set in concrete. As you stand in this position also think of lacing up across your back. Think of two vertical lines, each lying along the sacroiliac joints, and imagine these pulled in towards each other.

If you stay here for a while, you should begin to hurt – in fact, this exercise has been christened 'the pain exercise' by riders attending my workshops! You may feel it in your inner thigh, front thigh or outer thigh, but the best place to feel it is in those lines where you lace up. Keep repeating the exercise until this happens.

If the above does not work for you, buy a piece of relatively heavy exercise band (a thick, stretchy rubber band available from exercise studios and physical therapists), about 3ft long. Knot it into a loop, and put it just above your ankles. Now bend your knees, assume an 'on-horse' posture, and walk slowly. If you turn your toes in as you walk, you will feel the most stress in the muscles of your outside thigh. If you turn your toes out as you walk, you will feel the most stress in the 'lace-up' muscles across your back. If you do not feel anything for a while keep going until you do. Once you begin feeling your lower back, you will not want to keep going for long!

Your kitchen units may well be the right height for you to rest your lower back against the edge of the work surface as you think of narrowing in. You will feel the muscles across your sacrum bulk out against the units, and this gives such good feedback that it will hasten your learning process.

Chapter 9

Turns and Circles Demystified – An Introduction to Steering

▪ *Description of the ideal*

Good riders never think of steering the horse's nose, they think instead of steering his wither. They know that his nose will then go along in front of his wither, just as the wheel of a wheelbarrow goes along in front of the handles of the wheelbarrow. They also know that it is folly to pull on the inside rein, just as it is folly to pull on the inside handlebar of a wheelbarrow or a bicycle. Instead of thinking of their turning aids coming from their inside and outside legs and hands, they steer the horse between the 'V' shape of their thighs, so their turning aids are derived from their correct positioning, along with that of their seat bones and torso.

Very few people are naturally able to maintain a stable torso that does not lean and twist to the inside on a turn, and (on one rein in particular) this is an art that has to be learned, practised and refined over years. The rider can only control her body and the horse by honouring the laws of physics in the same way that an ice-skater does. The skater's or rider's torso must face to the **outside** of the turn, in the position of a fencing lunge, as if she is always riding along the tangent of the circle. If she puts a twist in

The collapse – seen from the back. Notice that the rider's inside leg–body angle closes, while the outer angle opens. usually the rider's inside seat bone is heavier, but some riders collapse like this while drawing up their inside seat bone.

her spine so that her shoulders face to the inside, she becomes very likely also to face her pelvis to the inside. But even if she limits the twist to her spine, it still creates the lean and collapse that make both an ice-skater and a rider lose control of the turn.

If the horse has any tendency to fall out, a turn or circle begins by thinking of bringing the horse's outside shoulder away from the wall, and the rider's outside aids dominate. It is as if they themselves make a wall, refusing to leave a gap that the horse's outside shoulder can fall out through. If the horse tends to fall in, the rider still thinks of balancing his weight between his two shoulders, and uses her inside thigh as barrier to stop him from falling in more.

▪ *Common starting points*

Pulling on the inside rein is the instinctive way to turn a horse, and is the default setting for all riders. More perceptive riders realise that when you do this one of two things happens: either the horse pulls on the rein against you, elongates the inside of his body and goes straight on, or he brings his head to the inside whilst his wither goes to the outside. I call this a 'jack-knife', and the hinge at the wither mirrors the way in which an articulated lorry (or eighteen wheeler) goes round a corner. Unlike the lorry, however, the horse does not follow his nose – he follows his wither. So the rider who is attempting to leave the track is left pulling the horse's nose to the inside whilst his body continues straight along the wall.

When the horse wants to fall in off the track and cut the corners, the novice rider is now tempted to pull on the outside rein, but this just brings his nose more to the outside as his body falls more to the inside. More experienced riders try to correct the problem by bringing their inside hand across the neck.

Many riders are fixated by the idea of creating a bend, and confuse a bend with a jack-knife. As the horse's shoulder falls out they are no longer steering his wither, but because they can see his inside eye, they are convinced that all is well. Most riders are aware that the horse falls in on one rein and out on the other, but do not appreciate that these two apparently

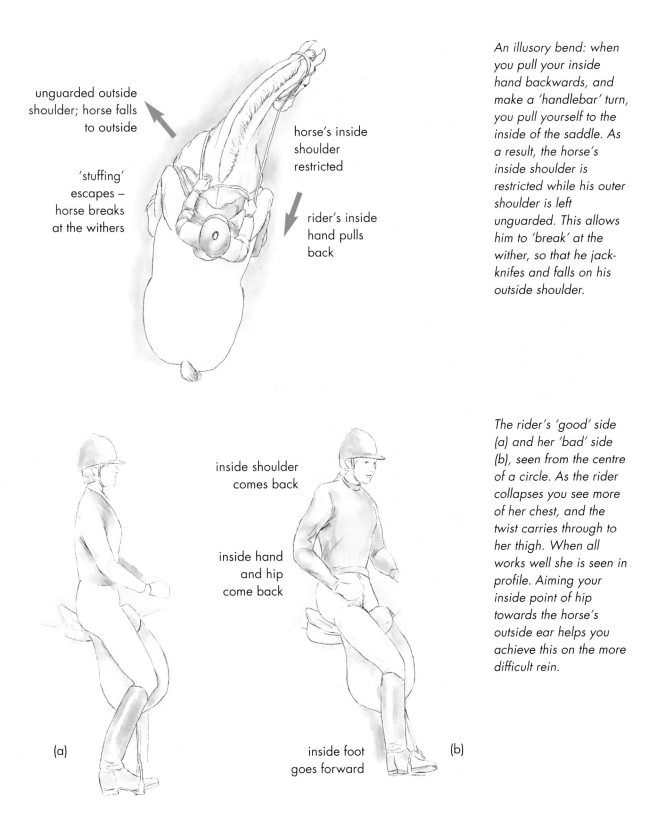

unguarded outside shoulder; horse falls to outside

'stuffing' escapes – horse breaks at the withers

horse's inside shoulder restricted

rider's inside hand pulls back

An illusory bend: when you pull your inside hand backwards, and make a 'handlebar' turn, you pull yourself to the inside of the saddle. As a result, the horse's inside shoulder is restricted while his outer shoulder is left unguarded. This allows him to 'break' at the wither, so that he jack-knifes and falls on his outside shoulder.

inside shoulder comes back

inside hand and hip come back

The rider's 'good' side (a) and her 'bad' side (b), seen from the centre of a circle. As the rider collapses you see more of her chest, and the twist carries through to her thigh. When all works well she is seen in profile. Aiming your inside point of hip towards the horse's outside ear helps you achieve this on the more difficult rein.

(a)

(b)

inside foot goes forward

different problems are just opposite sides of the same coin. Falling in is usually felt and diagnosed as a problem, whilst falling out is not. In reality, both are symptoms of the fact that the horse's weight is always being displaced onto one of his shoulders.

■ *The fix*

Forget the idea of bend and learn to steer the wither. Begin by diagnosing what actually happens on a circle in each direction, and imagine the line of a 20m circle drawn on the ground with a can of paint. Can you steer the horse's wither and forelegs along that line? What goes wrong on each rein? Does he fall in or out consistently, or does he change his tactics on different parts of the circle? You have to know what is actually happening before you can devise the correct tactics for dealing with it.

Get yourself out of the mind-set which presumes that your hands and lower legs can fix the problem. Think of steering the horse between the 'V' shape of your thighs, and imagine that pressure from your right thigh sends him left, whilst pressure from your left thigh sends him right. Then put on pressure with both thighs and send him down the middle of such a narrow corridor that he cannot move from side to side within it. Keep thinking of steering his wither along the imaginary line drawn on the ground, and try to keep your attention less on his nose.

If the horse is falling in, think of your inside thigh as if it were a power hose, or a weapon that sends light beams or laser beams streaming out through your knee. Then think of aiming those light beams in the direction you want to go. This can be easiest if you ride a square. As soon as you have turned a corner, aim at the point that will form the next corner. Briefly let off the aim to turn and immediately re-aim. Once you have become proficient on a square, adapt the same idea to the circle.

If the horse is falling out, you have to think of making a wall with your outside aids, so that there is no gap for the horse's outside shoulder to fall through. Unwittingly, you will find yourself advancing your outside hand, outside elbow and outside shoulder to accommodate the lengthening in the outside of the horse's body. As the turn fails to happen you will then almost certainly pull on the inside rein, which will send his outside shoulder even more to the outside. You are now twisted to the inside, and probably leaning to the inside as well. Keep your outside shoulder, elbow, hand, seat bone and thigh in the same (back) position, making them form the outside of the fencing lunge. Realise that this is where 'outside leg behind the girth' comes from, but that your lower leg positioning is the result of (and much less important than) your torso positioning.

Always keep in mind the idea of the horse turning like a bus, with his forehand turning around his quarters, in a way reminiscent of a turn on the haunches. This is the best way to programme yourself not to make him jack-knife and turn like an articulated lorry.

▪ *Troubleshooting – now*

Once things have already gone wrong it is too late to think of solving any problem in riding, and if you were riding a dressage test you would have lost marks already. You need to solve it **before** it happens, thinking ahead and positioning yourself as well as you can to mitigate it. You need to think about leaving the track well before you arrive at it, and to think about crossing the centre line well before you arrive there. Positioning yourself well can set up the next quadrant of the circle, but do not expect it to 'buy' you any more time than that.

When your horse falls in or falls out, does he speed up or slow down? Horses can do either as they fall out, and will usually speed up as they fall in. If you can keep his speed and tempo the same you can thwart some of his plans, and help yourself to hold him on the ideal line.

Realise that an effective correction for the horse who falls out keeps the inside of his body longer than you are used to. This is a surprise to people who are used to thinking about his inside being shorter because of the bend, and it may help you to ride thinking of counter flexion. It is not that you actually want the horse to look to the outside; it is just that you do not want him to look to the inside.

Catch yourself whenever you are tempted to pull on the inside rein, and realise that this is a symptom of other things that have gone wrong.

With crookedness in particular your subjective feelings are not to be trusted. When you counteract your natural symmetry, you will feel as if you have brought your outside seat bone so far back that you are facing way too much to the outside.

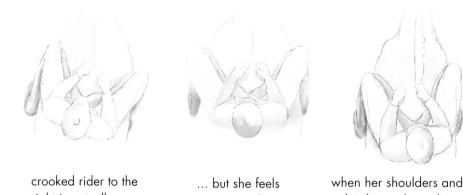

crooked rider to the right is actually placed like this ...

... but she feels symmetrical

when her shoulders and pelvis lie on the radius of the circle she is riding, she will feel like this

Have you lost your outside seat bone? Is it still in the back position? Think of keeping it far back and close to the horse's spine, realising that advancing your outside shoulder will inevitably bring your seat bone forward and off the saddle. Is your chin over the horse's mane, or are you leaning to the inside? You will maintain both your vertical alignment and the fencing lunge position more easily if you think of aiming your inside point of hip towards the horse's outside ear. This should help you to keep even weight on both seat bones, with your inside thigh and the tendon at the corner of your pubic bone lying more directly against the saddle.

As you 'sandwich' the horse to turn him, you have to have somewhere to push him round from (your outside seat bone) and something to push him into (your top inside thigh as it lies against the saddle). Your inherent asymmetry will make this far harder than it sounds, and if either of these components are missing, you will be in trouble, and will probably resort to your hand. Your asymmetry will cause you to tend to lose one seat bone, to twist and lean one way, and to take one thigh away from the saddle. You will have the biggest problems steering on the rein where you lean and twist to the inside, but if this is your habit, the correction that keeps you vertical will feel like such an exaggerated twist to the outside that you will be tempted not to make it. Get external feedback, if you can, from a friend or a video camera.

■ *Troubleshooting – on through time*

Appreciate that you now know that you should not pull on the inside rein, and understand how you create your own demise by doing so. But knowing this in theory will not stop you from pulling on it in practice, and this default setting **will** operate until you have something else to do instead. This 'something else' has been discussed in terms of the thighs, the outside

Common responses

These vary from:

'He just doesn't want to go where I want him to go.'

'I never realised before that the horse's nose and his wither go in opposite directions.'

to:

'I think I understand this now. So he falls in on the left rein and out on the right rein, which means that his weight is always displaced onto his left shoulder.'

'Help! I lost that outside seat bone again, and every time it happens I end up pulling on the inside rein...'

'I feel like I am facing way to the outside. Are you sure that this puts me in profile? It feels so exaggerated, but he does turn more easily when I can do it.'

and:

'I'm really getting the hang of this now. It feels so weird to think about counter flexion, but it keeps his wither much more on the correct line.'

'Ah yes, so he slows down every time he falls out. If I beat him to it, both with keeping him forward and with getting my pelvis in place, it's all so much easier. But I have to be thinking ahead.'

aids, fencing lunge position, and steering the wither – and these are powerful concepts. But the even-more-hidden dimensions of steering concern the corrections which enable the rider to position and stabilise herself over the horse's long back muscles. Understanding how your asymmetry operates will not in itself keep you symmetrical, but you must never give up the struggle to maintain the fencing lunge position, with equal weight on each seat bone and your chin over the horse's mane. Rest assured that your asymmetry will never go away, but that you can learn how to cope with it.

▪ *Test yourself – have you got it?*

You have got it when you can steer the horse's wither without being tempted to pull on the inside rein. In practice, there will inevitably be a point when you reach the end of your stretch zone, panic and resort to the default setting. But your aim must be to push the boundary of your panic zone further and further away. You are well on the way to getting it when you can give your inside hand away just at the point when you would have pulled on it, and can focus instead on re-finding the wall that will make your outside aids do their job.

You have got it when you realise how your body positioning contributes to, and perhaps even causes, the problems you experience with steering. If you think it is all your horse's fault, you most definitely have **not** got it.

▪ *Off-horse exercises*

If you can bear to sink this low, sit on a friend's back whilst she plays the role of your horse. Keep some of your weight on your feet, and be mindful of her plight! Without thinking much about it, turn her one way. Then analyse what you have done: you will almost certainly find that you turned your whole body (both shoulders and pelvis) in that direction, and that your horse swivelled about an axis, so that her shoulders and head move to the inside and her quarters to the outside. Repeat this several times to clarify the pattern.

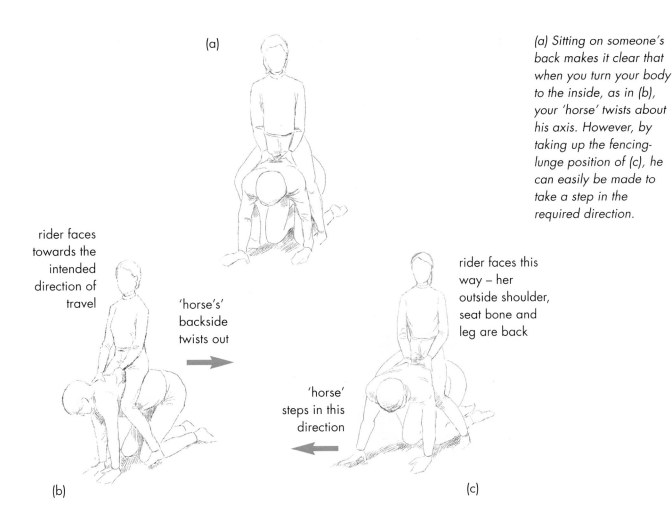

(a)

(a) Sitting on someone's back makes it clear that when you turn your body to the inside, as in (b), your 'horse' twists about his axis. However, by taking up the fencing-lunge position of (c), he can easily be made to take a step in the required direction.

rider faces towards the intended direction of travel

'horse's' backside twists out

rider faces this way – her outside shoulder, seat bone and leg are back

'horse' steps in this direction

(b)

(c)

Then, deliberately put yourself into position, with your inside leg underneath you and your outside leg back. Think of making a fencing lunge, as if you could push off your outside foot, and as if someone were pulling on your inside knee. Your 'horse' should find that she at least rocks in that direction, and ideally, she should move one of her front 'legs' in that direction. This exercise is very powerful, and should be experienced in the roles of both rider and horse.

Sit on a physioball with your feet more in front of you than they were in the balancing exercise in Chapter 6. Rest your hands on the top of your thighs, just as they meet your torso. Slowly lift each leg in turn, and then return it to the ground. Continue 'marching', but notice which leg is harder to lift, and how you tend to distort your ribcage as you do so. Ideally,

'Marching' on a physioball. Slowly lift one foot about 4 inches off the floor, and then lift the other foot. This is much harder than it sounds, and on one side at least, you will find your ribcage distorting. Can you work out what to do to stay straight?

perform the exercise in front of a mirror, or get feedback from a friend. Your torso will tend to distort in exactly the same way as it does when you ride, and the physioball is a fantastic mirror of the physical challenges of riding a circle. What do you have to do to hold yourself vertical and unmoved as you lift each leg? Practise on the ball until it becomes easier, and take these same corrections with you into your riding.

Chapter 10

Leg, Leg, Leg? – Lower Legs, the Physical Challenge.

■ *Description of the ideal*

The neutral position of the lower leg is determined by the vertical shoulder/hip/heel line, and the questions: 'How would you land on the riding arena if we took your horse out from under you by magic?' and 'Would you balance on a diving board?' Ideally, the heel is slightly lower than the toe, and aiming back towards the horse's hock, but it is sufficient to have the heel level with the toe. The foot rests lightly in the stirrup. Whilst the inside thigh and the top of the rider's boot must be on the horse, the lower leg hangs close to his side, but not on it. The leg remains still unless the rider decides to use it.

A leg aid is like a slap with the whole lower leg, done without the heel lifting or the toe turning out. The leg makes contact for only a moment before rebounding away from the horse's side, and a stronger aid is like a harder slap. Only in this way can the leg be used from the knee down without repercussions from the knee up.

■ *Common starting points*

One rarely sees a rider whose lower leg is well aligned, and many more riders have their lower legs too far forward than have them too far back. Most riders have heard that their lower leg should be 'on the girth', and whilst they have also heard the idea of the shoulder/hip/heel vertical line, they have not realised that these two ideas are mutually exclusive. This means that you have to consign one of them to the scrap heap (unless you think 'on the girth' means 'near the girth' and refers to a part of your leg towards the top inside of your boot. I have heard Continental riders assign this meaning to the phrase.)

Most riders are determined to push their heels down, and do so by pushing their lower leg forward and aiming their heels towards the horse's knees. They lose the shoulder/hip/heel vertical line, and opt to put their lower leg closer to the girth. With the foot so far in front of their backside, they cannot support their own bodyweight. Also, the strong pressure into the stirrup creates an equal and opposite force which straightens the knee and hip joints and sends the rider's backside up out of the saddle. With her lower leg 'on the girth' it lies so far away from the horse's side that she has to swing it back to use it. In addition, she often rotates the toe outwards from the knee and lifts the toe and heel.

Riders who have their lower legs further back and thus closer to the horse's sides use aids that are nudges or squeezes rather than kicks or slaps, and many, many riders give an aid every stride, as if they were asking the horse to take each stride. This frequent use of the leg trains the horse to be dead to it, especially as there is no price to be paid for not responding.

In rising trot the majority of riders get to the top of the rise by straightening the knee and pushing on the stirrup, which means that their foot swings forward as they rise and back as they sit. In its swing back it may well give an aid. Sometimes, the rider lifts the knee and heel as she routinely uses her leg on the 'sit'. In both cases, these aids are almost bound to be given on auto-pilot, and they are not likely to be aids which really mean business.

In sitting trot, the vast majority of riders cannot control their lower legs, which wobble about. Some riders cling on with them, but this is more commonly seen in canter. Riders who continually lose their stirrups often curl their toes up inside their boots, and as the horse goes faster they are more inclined to fall prey to this panicked reaction.

Few riders control their lower legs really well, so that they can keep them in the same place in all of the gaits, and choose either to give an aid or not. Even when one leg works well, the other is usually suspect. There are almost always differences in tone and strength in each leg, and one leg is the kicking leg, whilst the other, which has higher tone, remains more still.

▪ *The fix*

Doublecheck that your foot rests lightly in the stirrup and that you are not pushing down hard on it in an attempt to get your heels down. Be willing to forget about 'heels down' for a while (unless you are jumping, but even then, many people have too strong a pressure in the stirrup). Be happy if you can get your heel level with your toe when sitting in the correct alignment, and if this is impossible, do some stretching exercises for the calf and hamstrings (*For the Good of the Rider* has a useful selection). Prioritise the correctness of your alignment, the stillness of your leg, and the quality and frequency of your leg aids. Ask a friend how would you land on the arena if she could take your horse out from under you by magic, and if you would balance on a diving board.

Aim to keep your lower leg slightly away from the horse's sides, with your heel turned outward and your toes pointing towards his elbows. If you naturally tend to turn your toes out, be sure that your thigh is rotated in from the hip joint. Think of the heel being back, up and out – you might even think of the leg movement in the 1920s dance, the Charleston. Avoid rolling your weight onto the outside of your ankle, and instead keep it evenly over the ball of your foot.

Be sure that your kick is like a slap which touches the horse's side only briefly before it rebounds. This means that it is more about your calf than your heel. Remind yourself what a slap is by using your hand to slap your thigh, first lightly, then with more gusto. A determined leg aid makes a specific 'thunk' sound, which you will recognise when you do it right.

It may help to think of your lower leg like a wooden boot tree inside a riding boot; the boot tree has no flexibility at the ankle, so it cannot allow the heel to come up or the toe to turn out. It slaps as one unit. Also, check that you do not scrunch up behind your knee as you give an aid, since closing this angle rotates the toes back and out. Think of turning your heel out with a rotation that begins on the outside back of your calf just below your knee, and maintain this rotation as you kick.

Are you imagining that you have to ask the horse for every step, or are you imagining that you put him in gear, leave him to go, and then give him a reminder when he starts to 'rev down' (as he almost certainly will)? Asking for every step is like nagging at someone to get out of bed. The repeating conversation: 'You've got to' –'I don't want to' is no fun for either party, and in effect you have to rip the bed clothes off the horse and **GET HIM OUT OF BED**. You know yourself how much more fun you have once you have decided to get up and get on with your day, and so it is for the horse. When he threatens to get back into bed you respond by saying, 'Not with me you don't.' This means that the leg is used as a **prevention** (to stop him from revving down) rather than a **cure** (to make him take the next step).

Most riders use their legs in a predictable rhythm, and they are in fact training the horse to be dead to the leg, since it becomes like background music that he fails to notice. In fact, most riders have long ago become oblivious **themselves** to the way that they are using their legs, which means that rider and horse are each as 'tuned out' as the other. Since the horse pays no penalty for not moving forward in response to the leg, the rider is implying that his non-response is fine by her. You change this in the following way.

In walk, use one light slap with both legs, then use a heartier slap, and if the horse does not go forward more, use your stick just behind your leg. Allow the horse to go forward into trot or canter. Be sure that you are bearing down, and that you stay 'with' him, i.e. that you do not topple back. (Hold the mane or a neck-strap if necessary.) Come quietly to walk again, and when he slows down, test his response to a light leg aid. If he does not walk on, use the heartier slap and then your stick. Come back to walk and when he next backs off, test him with the light kick and repeat the process if necessary. You will be surprised at how few repetitions of this it takes for the horse to register your light leg aid and respect it. When the horse is walking well, be sure to **get off his case** and leave him to go. This is his reward. It is the contrast between when you use your leg and when you do not that puts the meaning back into the aid, and each leg aid must buy you at least a few strides in which you do not have to kick. The hard part is then to keep this new-found meaning in your leg aids, and not to regress back into rhythmic, predictable kicks.

How much 'clout' do you have with each leg? If one or both legs can kick only like a piece of limp lettuce then you need to work on the tone in that lower leg. How far down each leg do you feel solid and in control, as if your leg belongs to you? Few people feel in control all the way down to and within the foot on both legs. The challenges given in the off-horse exercises will help here, and you will need to do them repeatedly. Also refer to the dismounted exercise below, and then think of sticking out the tendons around your knee and your ankle, as this too will help to firm up the lower leg.

▪ *Troubleshooting – now*

If you are used to using your leg on 'auto-pilot', you will have to pay attention 100 per cent of the time, for as soon as you forget to notice, you will begin kicking again. If you cannot feel yourself kicking but a friend tells you that you are, exaggerate the kicking movements until you can feel them, and then alternate between deliberately kicking and keeping a genuinely still leg.

If you lack tone, and feel that your slap has no 'clout', you will find yourself attempting to make up for your weakness by lifting your heel, turning out your toe, bringing your foot back and using more prolonged nudges or squeezes. To stop yourself becoming this desperate, think of hitting the horse with the inside of the stirrup iron. After every leg aid, check that your leg has returned to its correct, neutral position, slightly away from the horse's side with the heel turned outwards. If all else fails, use your stick for a while instead of your leg, just to stop yourself from falling

Common responses

These vary from:

'What do you mean when you say that I'm kicking with every stride? I can't feel anything.'

'But I thought that I was supposed to use my legs alternately in walk. Are you sure that this will only deaden him?'

to:

'Oh my goodness, these leg aids work! I never knew that he could go forward like this.'

'It really is so much more fun when I don't have to nag him all the time, and I think he likes it better too.'

and:

'My right leg is doing great, but there is still a bit of a wobble down my left leg. I don't quite feel as if the ankle and foot belong to me. I can get it better for short periods of time, but it's never quite like the right.'

back into the old pattern. One nudge (like one cigarette) could be fatal.

You will have to keep checking the quality and the quantity of your leg aids, and catch yourself on this again and again. Do not let a lazy horse tempt you into using a more prolonged nudge or squeeze. Remember the dictum: if you don't mean it, don't use it, and if you use it, be sure that you mean it.

■ *Troubleshooting – on through time*

It is not easy to get still, stable lower legs, and to give effective leg aids, so you will probably be working on this for years to come. Keep being sure that it is **you** and not your horse who is determining the meaning of a 'go' aid. Are you and he both 'present' or are you 'spacing out'? The horse who is paying attention has his ears out sideways, and if the horse's ears are pricked he is admiring the view with little attention on you. Your lower leg is as much for getting his attention as it is for sending him forward. If he pricks his ears, kick, and aim to have his ears out sideways for progressively more of the time. Realise that with some horses, getting their attention is the hardest part of riding them. As ever, beware the rhythmic, predictable kick.

▪ *Test yourself – have you got it?*

How still can you keep your lower leg when you are not actually using it? Is the shoulder/hip/heel line easy to maintain? Which leg do you struggle more with? Few people find this easy, especially in sitting trot, so do not expect a quick fix.

Do you immediately notice when your horse backs off? What do you do about it? Suppose that the ideal is a 10 out of 10 in impulsion. Do you catch any 'winding down' on a 9 or a 4? This will dramatically change the finesse (or enormity) of your response, and the overall picture you create. You have to be one jump ahead of your horse, because once he has visibly slowed down the dressage judge saw it happen. The test is your ability to catch him and respond appropriately as the thought goes through his brain.

How much of the time do your have your horse's attention, with his ears out sideways?

▪ *Off-horse exercises*

Squat, with your backside close to your feet (hold onto something if necessary). Can you keep your heels on the floor? If not, there is some shortening of the muscles that form the back of the thigh (the hamstrings) and also the back of the calf. This shortening could even prevent you from getting your heel level with your toe when you are riding, and will only be mitigated by doing stretches.

Stand on one leg, place the other in an 'on-horse' position, and swing the calf slowly backwards and forwards from a still knee. If possible, position yourself so that you can see the movement in a mirror. Realise that as your foot swings forward your heel looks down, that as it swings back the heel looks up, and that in its neutral position the heel is probably level with your toe. But realise that nothing has changed in the ankle joint itself. This means that anyone can get their heel to look down by pushing the lower leg forward, but that it takes much longer calf muscles to get the heel to aim down and back towards the horse's hock. As long as you are holding the correct alignment and your calf muscles are under stretch, you are doing for yourself what the skilled rider does by having the heel aim down and back. If you had an ideal body your heel **would** be down, but it does not matter right now if it is not. Alignment is your most important priority.

Stand in an 'on-horse' position, and notice where on your foot your weight is taken. It is probably fairly evenly balanced between your heel and the ball of your foot. Gradually fold down into jumping position, moving your hand forward as you would over a fence. Where is your weight taken now? You will almost certainly find that it is more on your heel – in

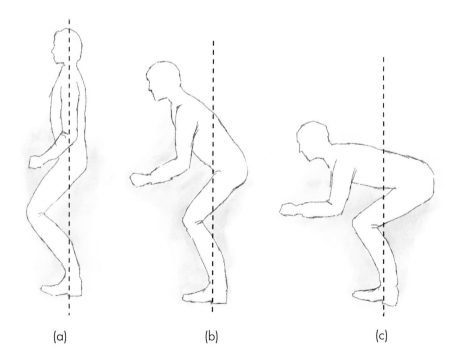

The rider's centre of gravity over her base of support: (a) 'on-horse' dressage line-up; (b) in one of any number of places in which she can be in balance before she finally reaches (c) and is folded down as she would over a fence.

(a)   (b)   (c)

fact, you can probably lift your toes off the floor and balance on the back edge of your boots. As you come up again, you will feel your weight roll forwards to be partially taken on the ball of the foot. This exercise beautifully demonstrates the difference between the flatwork balance and the jumping balance, and how weighting your heel requires you either to fold forward, or to 'water-ski', leaning back and counter-balancing your weight with the reins. If you cannot maintain a good flatwork balance and repeatedly find yourself in either of the above positions, your 'heels down' fetish might well be the cause.

Place your fingers around one ankle joint, realising that the large Achilles' tendon is at the back of it, and at the front of it are five long tendons that go to your toes. Stick out these tendons against your fingers, and notice that doing this makes your toes come up. Do this while riding, especially if you tend to curl your toes.

Put the fingers of each hand under one knee, and feel for the tendons that lie to the inside and outside at the back of the joint. Stick out these tendons against your fingers. If you find the tendon on the outside harder to activate, turn your toe out, and if the tendons on the inside are harder, turn your toe in. Also stick out these tendons when riding, aiming to keep your toes forward.

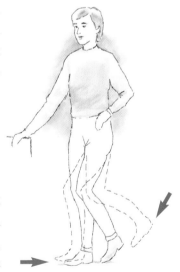

The 'dead leg' exercise in which you stick out the tendons at the knee and ankle whilst swinging your leg from the hip.

Hold on to something for support, and stand on one leg. Hold the other in an 'on-horse' position with your foot slightly off the ground. Swing that leg backwards and forwards from the knee, and also from the hip. Then, stick out the tendons around the ankle and knee (put your hand around them if necessary), and swing your leg from the hip. You should find that it is much less loose, and that it swings as one piece. This difference illustrates how sticking out the tendons increases the tone in your leg and enables you to hold it more still when riding. Repeat the exercise with the other leg, and discover which of them is harder to tone. Practise this often.

The following exercise is best done on-horse with a partner, but can be adapted to become an off-horse exercise by pushing your heel against walls, door jambs, and strong table legs. Again, it increases the tone in your legs. As your partner provides a resistance for you to push against, she needs to stabilise herself well. This is best done with feet apart, knees

Placing the body and arm to provide a resistance that the rider pushes her heel back into.

bent, and her elbow placed just to the inside of her point of hip. For a period of thirty seconds or more in each position you push your heel back into her hand, out into her hand, forward into her hand, and in against her hand (she will have to adapt her stance for this last one). Your lower leg should not move, and you need to take care not to roll your weight onto the outer edge of your foot. Be sure that you do not pop up, lean back, or distort your torso in any other way. As the partner, encourage the rider to push hard, and notice the strength (or lack of it) in each position. This exercise can make a huge difference to the solidity and stability of each leg. The pushes out and back are the most important to practise off horse.

Discovering a Contact –
Contact, and the
Walk/Halt Transitions

■ *Description of the ideal*

The contact is created by virtue of where the rider places her hand and the length of the reins, i.e. to 'take up a contact' does not involve a pull back. The hands remain still, and are held out in front of the rider as if she were 'pushing a baby buggy', or as if she were pushing the hands forward against a resistance. There is very little weight in the end of the reins, but the rider can feel the horse and the horse can feel the rider on a consistent basis. It is as if the reins were solid rods, forming the walls of a corridor on each side of the horse's neck, and as if the bit formed the lid on the end of a toothpaste tube, stopping the toothpaste (or stuffing) from leaking out of the horse. When the reins are loopy, the horse is always 'unstuffed' (see page 49, bottom diagram), and the skilled rider has learned to find the fine line between having no contact and restricting the horse by pulling back.

■ *Common starting points*

Some riders have misconceptions about how heavy the horse should feel in their hand, and imagine that they should be doing him the honour of holding his head up for him. The majority of riders know in theory that they should not have a heavy contact and/or a pull on the reins (and a few take this idea to such extremes that they have reins 'like washing lines'). But most riders pull at least some of the time, for pulling is the 'default setting' whenever humans are riding horses.

The desires to slow down, be in control, steer, and have the horse 'on the bit' all tempt riders to pull even more, but all of these ends can and should be achieved by other means. It is when the rider runs out of tools in her (skilful rider's) tool kit that she resorts to the default setting of pulling. A badly trained horse makes this much more likely, for he himself pulls. He expects the rider to pull back against him, and sets her up to do so. The expectation in either party that riding involves pulling tends to seduce the other party into pulling as well, creating a self-fulfilling prophecy.

Before we even consider the issues of slowing down, being in control, steering, and having the horse on the bit, the basic idea of going 'with' him presents problems, and few riders 'go with' the horse so well that their hand does not restrict his energy. To understand how this restriction creeps in, consider the rider doing sitting trot on the lunge. She usually sits reasonably well as long as she is holding on to the front of the saddle. But when she lets go and no longer has that pull (which acts from the front towards the back) she finds herself bumping backwards. Riders not on the lunge stop themselves from bumping back by resorting to an equivalent pull on the reins, and some do not even realise they are doing so. According to the laws of physics, this pull will be needed until such time as the rider creates instead a force within her body which acts **from the back towards the front**. Bearing down is the first stage of that force, and only 5 per cent of riders are doing it. By definition, the other 95 per cent who do not bear down (i.e. who have not stabilised their torso enough to have an 'independent seat') **need** that pull to stop themselves from bumping backwards. This means that they will pull even though they know in theory that they shouldn't. Bearing down is the hidden dimension of riding – a lack that shows up most clearly in the rider's default relationship to the reins.

There is yet another, possibly even more insidious dimension to the contact, and what the rider does with her hands. Most riders have learned to 'fiddle the horse's head down', and to think in terms of using their hand to get his head down rather than using their torso and thigh to bring his back up. These two strategies are worlds apart, and the horses show the differences between them.

▪ *The fix*

The essence of this is best described by showing you how to ride good walk/halt transitions. Learning to do these changes both the rider's and the horse's relationships to the bit, and provides the perfect illustration of how 'it takes two to pull'. Riding them well makes it very clear that when the rider refuses to play the game, the horse cannot play it either.

Since pulling is the default setting for riders, the fix has to be as much about what to do with your torso as it is about what to do with your hand. It will not work for me to assume that your body is already working perfectly, and to tell you what you what you would do with your hand if that were the case. This mistake is all pervasive in equestrian literature and in teaching, and it has thwarted your best intentions up to now.

Ride a few walk/halt transitions, and notice what you do with both your body and your hand. Ideally, work with a friend who can ask you these questions and help you become aware of their answers. How much do you pull? Do you need to pull, or is your horse the type who stops easily? (Perhaps he is so lazy that he is longing to stop, or perhaps he backs off the bit the moment he feels the rein. Or perhaps you already ride these really well!) Do you continue to bear down as you halt? What happens to your breathing? Do you grow up tall and pull your stomach in? Do you change the contact that your underside has with the saddle? Do you press harder in the stirrups? Do you lean back or lean forward? Do you round or hollow your back? Does your horse stop with clarity, or does he gradually wind down like a clockwork toy?

The key to using your hand correctly lies in stabilising your body. Even if it takes ten seconds for the halt to happen, you must **for that whole ten seconds:** bear down, remain vertical without growing tall, leaning backwards or forwards, and without hollowing or rounding your back. You

The horse that has been 'fiddled down' usually looks as if he has a large head that has been scrunched back into a short neck, and there is a tight inverted 'V' shape under the gullet. He may well be overbent, sometimes with a light or non-existent contact, and sometimes with a heavy one. He is unlikely to move as freely as he would if the rider's hand had not become a restriction.

In contrast, the horse whose back has come up, and who has been hung off his top line, looks so exquisitely 'right'. He exemplifies the ideals of dressage, and there is no sense of his head having been scrunched backwards by the rider. It is as if his neck reaches, arches, and grows out of his wither, with his head just hanging off the end of it. The underside of his jowl shows the more open shape of an inverted 'U'. He is poetry in motion.

must keep your feet light into the stirrups and your underside down on the saddle. The aid to halt is essentially that you stop your seat bones from moving whilst stabilising your torso, and you stop a horse much like you stop a trampoline. If you can do this, you are no longer playing your half of the game in the dismounted exercise below. How much you then have to do with your hand depends on how much the horse respects the bit.

The key to this is that the hand must offer the horse a passive resistance and not a pull. The differences between them, and also the quality of an ideal contact, are best appreciated by having a friend hold the reins close to the bit and play the role of the horse. Have her check that you are holding the rein as shown in the drawing opposite, with the holding happening primarily between your thumb and first finger.

As you first take up a contact, your partner needs to be sure that the contact is being created only by virtue of where you place your hand and the length of the rein. It must not involve a pull back – but since this is likely to be your habitual pattern, it probably will initially. If necessary, have her put her hands in front of your hands so that she gives you a resistance you can push your hands against. You must then reproduce that feeling as she holds the other end of the rein. Have your friend test you by repeatedly asking you to drop the reins and then to 'take up a contact'. You only pass the test when she is sure that there is no pulling involved. Then be sure that each of you can sense the presence of the other, so that the rein is not a loop. Here is your ideal contact.

Holding the rein, with the middle joint of the thumb up so that the rein is held by pressing the pad of the thumb on the first finger. Keeping the last joint of the fingers straight, rather than closed, helps to stabilise the rider and keep her from curling her toes.

Your partner then makes a pull on the reins, as your horse may have done in your attempts to halt. Your task is only to press harder with your thumb on the reins, whilst remaining vertical and bearing down. This is the passive resistance. You can make it more effective by thinking of your thumbs being connected to your wrists, your wrists to your elbows, your elbows to your shoulders, and your shoulders to your shoulder blades. Then think of these sliding down past your back in a 'V' shape that has its point at your waistband (following the shape of the trapezius muscle, shown in the drawing on page 67). Your partner should feel as if there is an anchor on the end of the rein, and you should feel that you are unmoved as she takes her hold. Rotate between the ideal contact, a passive resistance, and pulling. Feel how pulling changes the feeling in the rein, arm and hand (for both parties), and how it changes your torso too. The difference should be like chalk and cheese.

Repeat the halts, say, on a 20m circle, riding possibly four of them on each circle. Think of the passive resistance being the last phase of the halt aid. Stopping with your seat bones may be enough to stop the horse, or he may make a meal out of trying to make you pull. Be sure that you do not fall into any of the traps listed above, or he will erode your torso stability enough to succeed. It can help to make the sound 'pssst' as you halt, as this will ensure that you keep breathing out and bearing down. Also, be sure that your reins are short enough before you begin, otherwise you will draw your hand back to take up the slack, and the next thing you know, your passive resistance has become a pull.

A good halt is like an axe falling, or like a knife passing through butter. The horse moves from walking on to stopping without any winding down. Think of keeping a 'Superman' quality in your body. Do not let yourself become like Clark Kent just because you know you are going to stop. If you cannot get the halt to work well, check through all the possible mistakes listed above. Be absolutely sure that the line from your pubic bone to your belly button, sternum, and collar bone remains vertical. Think of pressing it against an imaginary plane of plexiglass. It is all too easy to lean back, and become a water skier to the horse's motor boat, at which point you are pulling, he is pulling, and he does not stop.

Think of it this way. If your horse is used to 'winding down' into the halt as both of you pull on the reins, he is expecting the bit to pull back against him. As you go to ride a good halt he will have the same expectation. But if you can hold your passive resistance the bit acts differently, as if it is a brick wall that does not pull back. He leans into the bit, as if he is saying, 'Come on, pull! You always pull, what's the matter with you?' He desperately wants you to pull, so that he can return to the status quo. But when you do not play his game, he eventually 'bounces off the bit', and halts by lowering his croup. Next time round, the process is repeated, but maybe he leans less hard for less long before he halts by 'sitting down'. Soon (if you can keep doing it correctly) he realises that he cannot seduce you into playing his game. He knows that the bit will always act like a brick wall, and that you will not pull back. In the halt, when he feels the bit, he bounces off it and immediately agrees to sit down.

This changes both his and your relationship to the bit – which now has become like neutral territory on which neither party is allowed to pull. Your aim is to maintain this in walk, trot and canter, and as you steer the horse and influence his carriage.

▪ *Troubleshooting – now*

Whenever the horse becomes strong in your hand, or speeds off with you, come back to the walk/halt transitions. These become the baseline for your correct interaction with the bit and the horse. Realise that the walk/halts are a microcosm of everything that can go wrong in riding, and that the mistakes you make here will be the mistakes that you make in the other gaits. How clearly can you identify your patterns? Do you round or hollow your back? Lean forward or lean back? Push into the stirrups, lift your backside and grow tall? These are very common mistakes, which all cause riders to pull. If your horse is heavy in your hand within the gaits, I will bet you any money you like that some of these patterns are operating in your body. **You will not change the quality of the contact without changing these first.**

What has to happen for you to lose your ideal contact? Can you keep 'pushing the baby buggy' if the horse speeds up? Whilst turning to both directions? What situations tempt you to pull, fiddle, carry your hands unevenly, drop them down, or saw with them? Do you come up with some other variations on the theme that I have not mentioned? Is there tension in your wrists or elbows? Test this by having a friend try to wiggle them. She should be able to, but if she feels that they are locked, try deliberately locking them and then letting them go as she continues to wiggle them. Make yourself aware of the difference between these two states, so that you will notice the next time that you lock them.

Even if you do not yet have the fix for each of these situations, diagnose yourself, and aim to push away the boundaries of the situations that tempt you to fiddle or pull.

■ *Troubleshooting – on through time*

When you lose the ideal contact what are you tempted to do with your hand? Whilst you might consider that your hand is being 'bad' for pulling or fiddling, realise that your hand is simply making up for what your body cannot do. It has a positive intention, and the challenge is to diagnose this and learn to fulfil it in another way. Is your hand trying to make the con-

---

Common responses

These vary from:

'But I've always been taught to lean back and become taller in a downwards transition.'

'Oops, I felt it that time. I grew tall and leant back. It's so hard to keep doing it right for all of those ten seconds. I start well, but then he gets me.'

'That worked better. I have to think of leaning forward, otherwise I lean back.'

to:

'I've got him! But he's still coming strongly against the bit, and the passive resistance has to be stronger than I had expected.'

'He's so much lighter now. It's as if he's suddenly agreed to this new arrangement, so my passive resistance is much less. I never knew that it could be this easy to stop.'

and:

'I'm getting so much better at "pushing the baby buggy". But I still catch myself grabbing at the rein when the horse speeds up, and fiddling his head down when he comes above the bit. Those panic reactions are just so hard to break.'

---

tact lighter, or to make it more definitive? Is it trying to help you steer the horse, or to shape him?

Realise that the ways in which you pull, fiddle, or move each hand, can be absolutely unconscious. If you look down at your hands they are likely to stop doing what they do otherwise (which makes it extra-difficult for you to become aware of how they move). Also realise that as you stop yourself from overtly pulling, you are likely to come up with more covert ways of doing it: you may pull by rounding your wrists, or by lifting or dropping them (relative to your thumb). You may start to hold the rein between your ring finger and little finger instead of between your thumb and first finger. Contrary to most people's expectations it is **long reins** which tempt riders to pull, not short reins. If you draw your hand back to take up the slack in the rein (or use one of the wrist-strategies described above to take up the slack) you are actually pulling. Every time you realise that this is so, check what has happened in your pelvis and torso, particularly with regard to bearing down. Realign yourself, bear down again, and try to make yourself 'push the baby buggy'. If you still feel that you **cannot not pull**, go back to walk/halt transitions, and check who is taking whom (as described on page 29). You will have to be in control of the tempo before you can give your hand forward.

If you are one of the few riders at the opposite end of the spectrum who has always ridden with the reins in loops, what will it take for you to take up a contact? Can you do so without leaning forward or rounding your shoulders? Many riders who ride with their reins too long are very unwilling to 'put a lid in the end of the toothpaste tube'. What is stopping you? Do you feel cruel, or just weird? Use the walk/halt transitions to help you do this, and realise that the horse is much better off knowing where your hand is than he is if he does not know when the rein will go loopy or tight. Get feedback from a friend about when you have a loop in the rein and when you do not.

At times when the horse puts slack into the rein it works well to widen your hands apart to take up that slack. By doing this, you keep the contact the same, and do not draw your hands either back or down (two common mistakes). At some stage, your hands will become so wide apart that you have to shorten your reins, but on an unsteady horse this can save you from continually having to lengthen and shorten them. Aim to keep the hand so that the lower arms and reins form a long thin triangle with an imaginary point just in front of the bit. It helps to imagine that you have only upper arms, and that you hold the reins as if your hands were at your elbows. Keep being sure that you **know in your elbows** if the reins are loopy or tight.

■ *Test yourself – have you got it?*

Can you ride good, 'clean', walk/halt transitions one after another, preferably on a variety of horses (who will test you in different ways)? If you can, your body has understood the difference between a passive resistance and pulling.

Imagine that we take 100 per cent of your attention and split it into two parts. What percentage would be on your hand, the rein contact, the position of the horse's head, and whether his nose is vertical? And what percentage would be on your pelvis and torso, the contact that your underneath makes with the saddle, and the shape of the horse's back (as a hollow, a flat surface, or a mound)? Remember, these two figures must add up to 100.

A vast percentage of riders have over 80 per cent of their attention on the rein contact and the need to have the horse's nose vertical. With only 20 per cent of their attention on their pelvis and torso and the feeling of the horse's back, they will spend a lifetime blinking and missing the secrets of good riding. These percentages have to be reversed for the rider to gain the skills (bearing down, plugging in, etc.) that make her body mechanics so influential that she will not feel the need to 'do things' with her hands. When that need drops away, she has got it.

Changing the focus of your attention can be the biggest challenge that faces you in your learning, especially if you have been made to feel paranoid about not having the horse on the bit.

■ *Off-horse exercises*

Stand opposite a partner, preferably someone of similar height and weight, and join hands. Now lean back against each other so that both of you are pulling. Either one of you could consider herself the rider and say of her partner, 'This horse just won't stop pulling. He ought to know by now!' But your partner (the horse) would be equally justified in saying, 'This rider just won't stop pulling. She ought to know by now!' The truth is that both parties need each other, and balance each other like two sides of an equation. But the moment one of them brings her body upright, takes a step back, and takes responsibility for her own bodyweight, the other partner has to do the same. It really does take two to pull – but only one to stop the game. Since you are the rider, and the more intelligent partner, it has to be you. Take this lesson into your walk/halt transitions, and remember it every time the horse becomes heavy in your hand.

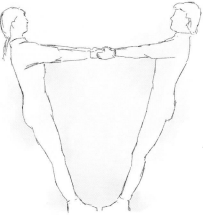

When two people hold hands and lean back against each other, they show a similar dynamic to the rider and horse who both pull. The only solution is for one partner to take a step back and make her body vertical. This forces the other to follow suit.

I use an exercise with riders that takes this idea one stage further. I ask the rider to put both reins in one hand, and to hold the other as if she is holding the rein. Then I curl my fingers around her fingers and gradually begin to pull on her arm, making sure that her elbow stays bent. I assure her that I, as the horse, can keep making this pull forever, and ask her how she is going to extract herself from her plight. Most riders soon realise that they will have to give their hand forward, making me step back to stop myself from falling over. Having made me take responsibility for my body-weight, they return their hand to its neutral position. But the mistake that many riders make is to snatch the hand back, and there they are, pulling again ...

The hand must come back into place making an ideal contact, even if the rider can only maintain this for a short time before she finds herself pulling again. Then, she has to give her hand towards the horse's mouth, making sure to put a loop in the rein. She has to maintain this for the time it takes for both of the horse's forelegs to take a step, and then be extremely careful as she replaces her hand. She is repeatedly saying to the horse, 'I won't play, and I'm not so daft as you think. You're going to have to hold up your own head.' It is vital that she is plugged in, bearing down and stabilising her torso as she gives her hand away, so that she gives **only her hand and not her body** (or her other hand). Doing this repeatedly can, like the walk/halt transitions, reform both the rider's and the horse's relationships to the bit.

Chapter 12

An Independent Seat – Matching the Forces Acting on Your Body

■ *Description of the ideal*

The rider who can match the forces which the horse's movement exerts on her body appears to sit still and do nothing. Although she is stabilising her body using high muscle tone, she is commonly thought of as being relaxed. She has an independent seat, and can give her hand forward, for she does not need her hands to stop herself from bumping backwards. Neither does she feel the need to restrict the horse's power with her hand, for she knows that control is control of **tempo**, and that she can only slow down the horse's legs by slowing down the speed of her seat-bone movement. Walk and then rising trot are the easiest gaits in which to match the forces and control the tempo. In a good rising-trot mechanism, the rider's thrust forward in each rise matches the thrust of the horse's hind leg. The fact that she makes a movement to match the forces makes this task easier, and it is (for most people) harder to do so in sitting trot and canter. Her body becomes like a metronome, and since she is moving in a certain tempo she gives the horse no choice but to trot in that tempo underneath her. The same principle holds true in sitting trot and canter.

■ *Common starting points*

A remarkable number of riders on forward-going horses are being run away with at walk, although mostly they do not realise that this is happening (they do, however, realise once they get into trot or canter!). Whenever the horse's legs speed out from under the rider and he 'takes her', she is likely to end up hanging onto the reins, and in the heat of the moment she forgets that this will make her horse claustrophobic. Sanity only prevails when she slows down her seat-bone movement (as discussed in Chapter 3) so that she 'takes him'.

In rising trot, few riders show good mechanics through which they match the thrust of the horse's hind leg whilst maintaining control of the tempo. Many riders have been taught to 'keep the rise tidy' by minimising it. When they do not match the thrust of the hind leg in each rise, one of two things happens:

1. The **phlegmatic horse** minimises his thrust to match the rider, and trots with far less power than he is capable of. If the rider kicks more, it will make little difference, for he is obeying her body's dictum to minimise the trot.

2. The **whizzy horse** is not so easily put off from going forward. Whenever he thrusts more than the rider, it is as if he has pulled the rug out from under her feet in that step, with the result that her centre of gravity is behind his. He is now towing the rider along, for she is no longer 'with him'. He reacts to this by maximising the discrepancy, and in effect, he plays the role of a motor boat in response to her playing the role of a water-skier. If the rider panics, and leans back and/or thrusts less in her attempt to slow the horse down, she too maximises the discrepancy. It is as if the rug is on a polished floor, so the more she leans back, the more the horse shoots out from under her. At the same time, his legs begin to move faster, leaving her even more out of control of the tempo.

This mechanism also explains why it is so important not to lean back in those walk/halt transitions – as well as in every other transition – and how

The water-skier/ motorboat scenario. The more the rider leans back, pulling on the reins and pushing into the stirrups, the more the horse speeds out from underneath her.

easily horse and rider can set up the counter-balance described in the dis-mounted exercise given in the previous chapter. The water-ski/motorboat scenario has lethal effects, for the rider who is (according to her instincts) saying 'whoa, whoa' is (according to the horse's instincts) saying 'go, go'.

■ *The fix*

In all of the gaits, you match the thrust of the horse's hind leg more effec-tively when you can lace up across your back, and begin your bear down in your back. (See Chapter 6.) If you ride a forward-going horse it is vital that you can control the tempo in walk before taking the faster gaits, oth-erwise you have no hope. You have to perfect the art of slowing down the movement of your seat bones, and plugging in, so that you become the prime mover, i.e. you move the horse instead of the horse moving you. Revisit Chapter 3, page 28, on plugging in, for more ideas that will help.

The biomechanics of the correct rise. The torso is like a block that is levered up over the pommel of the saddle by the thighs, and the angle between the leg and the body opens at each rise. The angle of the upper body changes from being inclined slightly forward in the sit to being vertical in the rise, so that the rider comes close to having a vertical line from her knee to her hip (the greater trochanter of the femur) to her shoulder. She must not take her hips in front of that point, which would place her upper body behind the vertical at the top of the rise.

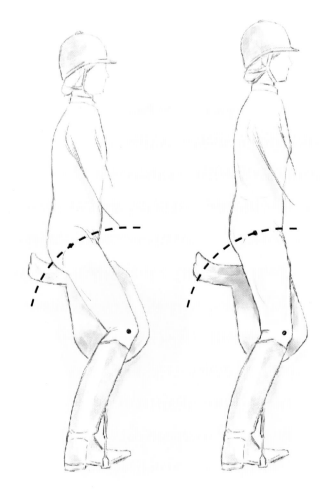

A correct rising-trot mechanism is vital if you are to match the forces acting on your body and also control the tempo in trot. In rising trot the knee acts as the centre point of a circle. The thigh bone is like the radius of that circle, and the bony knobble at the top outside thigh (the greater trochanter of the femur) describes an arc of a circle. During both the rise and the sit, nothing from the knee down changes, and there is barely any more weight placed in the stirrup.

However, most people rise by pushing in the foot and straightening the knee, and this is a habit that dies hard. It cannot be changed without your initial alignment being correct, giving you the balance over the stirrup that mirrors a diver's balance on a diving board. Be sure that you can balance out of the saddle at the top of the rise when standing still, with most of your weight taken on your thigh and knee, and little weight in your foot.

This could require significant effort on your part.

As you go to trot, be sure that every rise gets to this point, without your foot moving forward, and without more weight going into it. When you are beginning to establish this, ask yourself whether your midline, from your pubic bone to your belly button and sternum lengthens as you rise or stays the same. What happens as you sit – does it shorten or stay the same? Your goal is to keep it the same in each case, but you are almost bound to find that it lengthens as you rise, which lifts your chest (and probably your chin) whilst hollowing your back. This means that you are pulling yourself up with your chest and abdominal muscles – much as the horse who is on his forehand pulls himself along by lengthening his stomach muscles, lengthening his chest and the underside of his neck, and lifting his chin. I call this 'lengthening his underside', or 'taking underside steps'. In traditional language, both you and your horse are 'above the bit', and the cure for both of you lies in pushing yourselves along with your hind legs, whilst keeping your stomach muscles short so that your back does not hollow. Your horse then lengthens his topside, or takes 'topside steps'. He takes his cue from you, so by fixing your own movement pattern, you begin to fix his.

This is easier said than done. Think of your torso as a block, that is levered to the top of the rise by your thighs. Only then can you keep bearing down as you rise, for if you lengthen your stomach you will pull it in. Imagine someone's hand placed on your sacrum, pushing you up to the top of the rise. Also (this comes with my apologies for making you think such a gruesome thought) imagine a hook that dangles down from the sky in front of you, grabs you by the pubic bone, and heaves you up over the front of the saddle. If you were heaved up over it from this low down, your stomach muscles would not have to do anything to get you up there. They could simply keep bearing down.

When you land in the saddle, what direction do your seat bones point in? Most riders find that they point back, indicating that their back is hollow. With their backside sticking out behind them, they inevitably land towards the back of the saddle, and feel that they are immediately catapulted out of it by the horse. This means that they cannot make a pause and control the tempo, for this requires that you land with your backside under you. If you hollowed in the rise this is next to impossible, so imagine wearing an old-fashioned man's shirt with a long shirt-tail that passes under your backside. You could then pull on it to get to the top of the rise, and keep pulling on it to keep you landing with your backside under you and towards the front of the saddle.

In walk, be sure that your seat bones point down, and use your fingers to trace the line where the back of your backside contacts the saddle. Notice that if you hollow your back, there is probably at least an inch less of it in contact. When you land in the saddle in rising trot, that extra inch must still be in contact. In walk, notice too that your pubic bone is higher up than your seat bones, lying on the slope towards the pommel. When you land in trot it must still be higher, but it is likely to slide back down that slope so that it lies on the same level as your seat bones, which would then point towards the back.

Think of landing up the slope towards the pommel of the saddle, and in front of the dip in the horse's back. Feel your underneath land in the saddle, and think of making a pause or a velcro close in each landing. This is the only effective way to slow the tempo on a speedy horse (remember that pulling on the reins will make you become like a water-skier and him become like your motor boat). Once you have done it, if only for one sit, you will know that you have succeeded. It is a very distinct feeling that is immediately effective as the horse pauses with you.

▪ *Troubleshooting – now*

Many riders who round their back in walk actually hollow it in rising trot. Are you one of them? If so, be sure you appreciate that this change in your baseline requires a completely different set of corrections.

Almost everyone's natural pattern is to lengthen their front as they rise, and you will benefit by returning to the kneeling exercise (pages 62-63) before you read any further. Think of keeping your chest and knees closer together as you rise, with your knees staying in the same place on the saddle. Keep being sure that your kneecap points more down as your thigh rotates over your knee. Is your foot really staying still? Expect to feel strain in your thigh muscles, on the inside and/or front of them, and if you are not feeling this, start worrying! Keep adding to the strain by catching yourself when the weight goes back into your feet. You must keep it in your thighs, which must remain on the saddle. If they do not feel strong enough to support you, work in short bursts.

Round-backed riders sometimes shorten their front as they sit, giving way beneath their sternum and becoming 'C' shaped. Do you make this mistake as well as, or instead of, lengthening your front? A small percentage of riders tuck their backside under as they land and point their seat bones too forward. The vast majority tend to point them back. Which is your tendency?

Are your upper inside thighs on the saddle as you land? If you are rounding your back they may not be, and you will not succeed in changing your pelvic alignment without changing this. Do you 'pop yourself up' and clench your backside as you sit? It is imperative that you can feel your seat bones, and that you know which direction they point in. Do you tend to deaden the trampoline as you land, coming down heavily and squashing the horse, or does he throw you up before you feel you have really landed? This is the more common pattern, but suspect the former if you have diagnosed yourself as a heavy 'down' rider (see page 65) who tends to be too wide, and if you have trouble getting your horse to go forward. Think of landing lightly and quickly in the saddle, and imagine that a drawing pin (or push pin) will prick your backside if you land heavily.

If you tend to squash the horse on landing, you probably do not do a good job of controlling your descent into the saddle. Think of the thigh like a lever: the weight acting at the knee end must counterbalance the weight of your upper body – like one of those old-fashioned level crossing gates where a lump of concrete on one side of the support counterbalances the weight of the arm on the other. You, however, have the weight of your upper body stacked up on the end of the lever arm, so a lot of weight must act down by your knee. This counterbalance is stressful work! You have to **know** that you are doing it.

If, on the other hand, you are a rider who is catapulted out of the saddle the moment you land, you need to perfect the art of the 'velcro close sit'. This enables you to spend as long in the saddle as you do in the air, but it can prove elusive at first. Keep being aware of how your underneath comes down in the saddle, and really feel this on each landing. Once your seat bones point down it becomes possible to make a pause and thus to make the horse pause under you. Beware, however: typically, when riders think about this pause they let the rise go 'soggy' so that it does not have enough thrust and does not get to the balance point. Similarly, when they think about thrusting and getting to the balance point, they forget about the pauses. You need to find enough 'brain space' to process both ideas at once. You must thrust every thrust and land every landing. A motor-boat type of horse will not forgive you for either mistake, even if you make it only once.

To what extent do you open the angle between your leg and your body

---

Common responses

These vary from:

'I feel as if I'm going to the moon and back in each rise. Surely this can't be right?'

'It's not so difficult to stop myself from pushing up from my feet, but it's hellish hard not to lengthen my front.'

to:

'You're right, my weight did just go back into my feet. I think my thighs are giving out!'

'I felt it! That was the velcro close, and it really slowed him down.'

'I got him that time! As he hit the long side he wanted to pull the rug out from under my feet, but I was ready for him and kept matching him.'

and:

'It's so much harder to get a good rising-trot mechanism in my right side. I know I need to kneel down that leg more, but it's so hard to do.'

---

as you rise? Riders with short muscles at the front of the body and the thigh tend to rise without changing the angle of the upper body, and also to lean too far forward in the sit. If this happens to you, think of keeping a bigger distance between your chin and the horse's ears. Also, think of your pubic bone leading the way to the top of the rise, and imagine someone floating along behind you who has their hands on your shoulders and is drawing your shoulders back.

Realise that as you do rising trot, your elbows have to move so that your hands can stay still. If your elbows do not open and close with each rise and sit your hands will go up and down with you. If you need to, have a friend put her first finger within your hand, parallel to and right by the rein as you hold it. Then rise and sit, seeing if your hand pulls on her finger. By letting your elbow open as you rise you can ensure that this will not happen.

■ *Troubleshooting – on through time*

Ninety-five per cent of riders do not thrust enough in rising trot. The remaining 5 per cent thrust too much. This is most likely to happen if your horse is lazy, and you (as a 'pingy' sort of person) are feeling rather desperate about getting him going. Limit the rise by not letting so much of your thigh escape from the saddle. Kick or hit to get him forward, and do not let him delegate all the effort of thrusting to you. Take a video, still it at the top of the rise, and notice if your hips are in front of your pelvis.

The pattern of lengthening your front as you rise can be very ingrained and insidious. Its most dangerous aspect is the lengthening that occurs between your belly button and your pubic bone, for elongating from the belly button downwards predisposes you to hitting your crutch on the pommel. Added to this, sucking your stomach **back** as you simultaneously attempt to thrust your pelvis **forward** makes you look as if you are treading on the brake and the accelerator both at the same time. The horse tends to go as if he has brakes on too, so this is a profound way of becoming your own worst enemy. Do everything in your power to ensure that you are bearing down and keeping your front short as you rise.

Be sure that you keep the feeling of kneeling up and down as you rise. It is easy to get sloppy and lose this. Do your knee and foot stay in the same place throughout, with your kneecap pointing down more as you rise?

Which side of your body works better? Almost everyone finds that one leg forms a much better lever arm and keeps stacked up much better than the other. Does one knee tend to come up and one foot come forward so that you land in the armchair seat on that side? Is one knee less stable than the other? Do you land equally heavily on each seat bone, whichever rein you are riding on? Your asymmetry will begin to show up much more in trot, and you may need more information before you can do a good job of counteracting it. At the very least, become aware of it, and do the best you can on the more difficult rein. Keep thinking: knee down, foot back, land light.

▪ *Test yourself – have you got it?*

Be sure you know if you yourself tend to make your horses more dead or more 'pingy', and realise that your task is to cultivate the tonal quality and the mechanics that enable you to bring all sorts of different horses to just the right quality of 'trampoline bounce' in their trot. You have got it when your body is such a good metronome that you can hold the tempo (and the ideal quality of 'bounce'), whilst steadying speedy horses and motivating lazy ones. You need to feel that your rising trot mechanism is close to infallible.

Consider the idea that you get run away with from the moment you **decide** that you are being run away with. This is the moment at which you 'bail out' of attempting to match the forces acting on your body (which is forward riding) and resort to pulling on the reins (which is backward riding). You have got it when you can go faster than you really wanted, but can still match the horse, stay calm, and act as if it was your idea! With this attitude, you will be able to slow the tempo without becoming a water-skier and escalating the horse's run-away tendencies.

Off-horse exercises

Watch videos of riders like Reiner Klimke, Kyra Kyrklund, and Isobel Werth. Analyse their rising-trot mechanism according to the mechanics laid out here. How do they differ from most of the riders you see around you?

Repeat the kneeling exercise from Chapter 7 (pages 62-63), realising how well this illustrates the difference between lengthening your front as you rise and levering yourself up from your thighs. Note that in rising trot you are slightly inclined forward as you sit. This takes some of the strain off your thighs (and makes rising trot easier than this exercise), but I recommend that you do the exercise keeping your body vertical.

If you have had Alexander lessons, note the similarity to 'chair work', and realise that people tend to heave themselves out of chairs with their chin leading and their front lengthening. Few people naturally lever themselves up with their thighs, just as few horses naturally push themselves along from their hind legs. The temptation to try to get strength from lengthening the muscles of the stomach, chest and neck (which I call 'extension pattern') seems almost universal in both people and horses. Good movement draws on the strength of the core muscles of the torso and the hind legs. The front/underside of the human/horse then stay short (in 'flexion pattern'). This is much more effective, and much less damaging to the body.

Chapter 13

On the Bit? –
Shaping the Horse

▪ *Description of the ideal*

When the horse is working 'on the bit' and showing the biomechanics of correct movement, he will both look, move, and feel like the archetypal dressage horse. Whatever his conformational faults, he looks in proportion and 'all of a piece'. His body can be thought of like a strung bow (see Chapter 4, page 41), or like a suspension bridge, where the stanchions are the wither and the croup. His spine is like the roadway, and the ligaments which join the spinal processes are like the wires that hold up the bridge. Thus the middle of the back is drawn both up towards the wither, and up towards the croup. When the whole ligament system works well, it pulls the tail up into an arc, and the crest up into an arc. It is as if the whole of the horse's body is hung off his top line, leaving his legs free to move. This creates much more organised gaits than he has if his back is soggy or locked up, and as a result he is much easier to sit on. This makes it easier for the rider, who in turn can make it easier for the horse, whose improvement makes it easier for the rider, and so on, creating 'the spiral of increasing ease'.

In a biomechanically correct movement pattern, the horse's hind legs

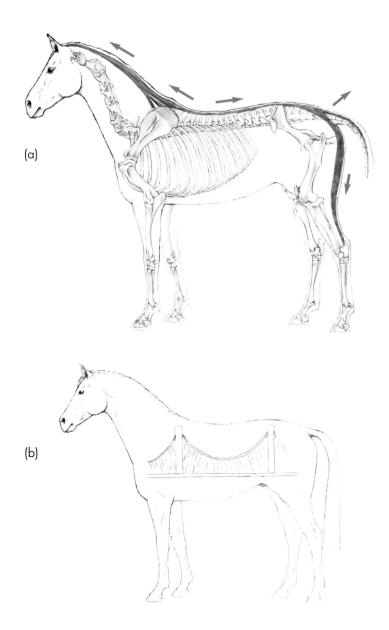

(a)

(b)

The ligament system which holds up the back. Ligaments (unlike tendons) are elastic, and they can be stretched by changes in the horse's carriage. The dorsal ligament of the neck attaches into the front of the poll, and as the horse lowers his head, the ligament stretches and then pulls on the spines of the withers. These in turn pull on the spines of the thoracic vertebrae. The supra-spinous ligament, which is a continuation of the dorsal ligament, begins just before the end of the thoracic spine, extending backwards over the croup and the sacrum and on down to the tip of the horse's tail. A further ligament system runs from the croup to the point of the buttock, and then down to the hock, where it joins with the Achilles tendon. (This includes the semitendinosus muscle, which functions as a ligament.) When the horse 'sits down', flexing the lumbo-sacral joint at the croup, the middle part of the spine is pulled up and back. When he reaches his head and neck forward, the spine is pulled up and forward. These two pulls lift the middle of the back, holding it up in the same way that the cables of a suspension bridge hold up the centre of the bridge. The stanchions of the bridge are the withers and croup, as shown in (b).

push him along, and that 'push' connects through his body without being jammed up, deadened, dissipated or deviated. That connection is created as the horse bears down (just like the rider), shortening his abdominal muscles as they form the string in the bow, and without this, his front and hind ends can act as two disconnected parts. The impulse of the 'connected' horse passes through a circuit, composed of the muscle chain on each side of the horse's spine and crest. From his hind legs, it passes over the points of the buttocks, over the croup, along the long back muscles and up his neck to his ears. The horse is then often said to be 'through' or 'working over his back'. The muscles function like elastic bands under tension, or as if water is 'whooshing' through hoses that have no blockages, kinks or leaks in them. However, this energy circuit is only complete when the rider too does not deaden, dissipate, or jam up that impulse. So the impulse can also be considered to pass from the horse's poll to his mouth and the bit, through the rider's hand, wrist, elbow and shoulder to her back and thus to the horse's back.

Many top-class trainers consider that the rider is 95 per cent responsible for the picture one sees when looking at the ridden horse. Yet the rider who is creating this beauty appears to sit still and do nothing. In reality, all of the co-ordinations described so far contribute to it, and the rider's thought process as she interacts with the horse is also paramount.

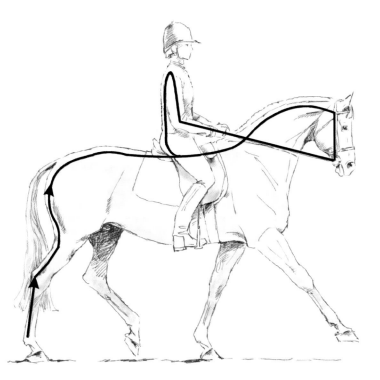

The complete circuit: the impulse from the horse's hind legs is transmitted through the horse's and the rider's bodies, without being blocked or dissipated.

▪ *Common starting points*

Many riders are searching for the ideal dressage horse, and whilst a horse will only be competitive if he has big powerful gaits and lots of presence, few people realise that any horse with reasonable conformation can be good to learn on. A horse should not be rejected just because he has (say) a long back or a big head. When he works 'through' these faults will not be visible, and it is his **attitude** which makes him more or less easy to learn on. When buying horses, discretion can be the better part of valour, and until you have the skills to match the power of a big, scopy horse, you are better to buy a horse appropriate for your skill level **now**.

At the expensive end of the spectrum many riders are over-horsed, and it is a myth to imagine that you can buy a trained horse, get on, press button B, and produce wonderful work. The horse can only perform up (or down) to the level that he is ridden. As the female partner in a couples dance pair, you can only dance as well as your male partner, and dancing with a good partner is a wonderful experience. But if you change partner and find yourself out of synch with your new beau, you cannot have the same good experience, however hard you try. He is pushing whilst you are pulling, and you 'read' each other so badly that the joy of the dance is lost. If you were a horse, your partner might be thinking, 'I paid £/$---- for this horse, and he's supposed to be trained, but look at how badly he dances!' But the horse cannot revert to his former style of 'dancing' any more than you can.

At the lower end of the market, some riders have not recognised that their horses are actually diamonds in the rough, whilst others have not recognised that their horses – whilst not actually lame – are severely compromised by injury or stress (as more expensive horses can be too). To have any chance of working 'through', these horses need extensive body-work, e.g. physiotherapy, massage or chiropractic, etc., which must be performed under veterinary guidance.

Whatever their make, shape, athleticism, and monetary value, our horses are able to read us riders like a book. They know how stable we are, how determined we are, and how asymmetrical we are, and they evolve their evasive patterns around our weaknesses. They tolerate being scrunched by our front-to-back, hand-dominant riding, but flourish when we gain the skills to draw their back up, and no longer need to stabilise ourselves or manipulate them with our hands. Sadly, it takes an enormous amount of training before we gain these skills, and also become able to 'read' them as well as they can 'read' us. Most riders have some other agenda, that may concern being in control, looking good, having the horse's head down, or winning – and very few riders have made learning how to ride well their top priority. This may be because so little constructive help has been available to show them how to bring the horse's back up instead of bringing his head down. But times are changing.

■ *The fix*

The essence of the fix is the change in your philosophy of riding that turns you from a 'head down' (i.e. front to back) rider to a back up (i.e. back to front) rider (see also page 92). Learning the skills that bring the horse's back up is a secondary issue, for it is all but impossible to teach them to someone who is fixated on his head position. You must somehow persuade yourself to **let go of that agenda** before you become available for new learning. When you have been harangued by previous teachers and feel that it is more than your life is worth to be seen with your horse's nose in the air, this is no easy task.

If you have worked diligently through the previous sections of this book, magic may already have happened. Often, aligning the body well, bearing down, plugging in, getting your weight down through your thighs, and getting the horse's attention is enough to dramatically change his carriage in walk. Riding good walk/halt transitions can also help with this. Changing his carriage in trot requires a good rising-trot mechanism, which incorporates each of the above elements into the way in which the thigh rotates about the knee. The rider must hold the horse's attention as well, and be taking the horse, but with a significant amount of energy (or water) powering round the circuit. This makes the energy flow less vulnerable to being blocked, deadened or dissipated.

Have someone knowledgeable do a belly-lift on your horse (first in the stable and later with you mounted). She does this by placing her fingertips on the midline of his belly just behind the girth, and jiggling them, pressing into him hard if need be. She needs to stand out of the way of his hind legs, and watch in case he kicks. Both she and you need to notice if his back lifts, and you may need to repeat the lift several times before it does. When you are mounted, the difference between 'up' and 'down' gives you a contrast that shows you what it means to have the back up – and for many riders, this is their first experience of feeling it change. Very few horses do not respond at all to a belly-lift, and, metaphorically speaking, their bodies are set in concrete. So if, when you try the lift unmounted you get no response, get your horse assessed by a bodyworker.

Label your horse's maximum 'up' as a 5, and his maximum hollow as a 0, and as you walk on, notice if his back lifts, drops or stays the same. As you pass each dressage marker, say out loud the number that represents the state of his back in that moment. Realise that it is not important to be objectively accurate; the point is to notice the difference between what you have decided to call a 2, a 3, and a 4. So do not think too hard; give the numbers 'off the top of your head'. This is important, for having a discussion inside your head about the number you should say takes time in which you are not interacting with your horse and not noticing what is happening. If your final decision comes late, it may no longer be relevant. This dialogue with yourself absents you from dialogue with your horse, and you have substituted the kind of thinking that may work in the academic world, but does not work well with horses or in sporting performance of any kind.

As you do this exercise, do not concern yourself about a 5 being good, and thus a case for euphoria and congratulations, or about a 2 being bad, and perhaps a cause for disappointment and self-abnegation. Just simply notice, in a non-judgemental way that cuts out any commentary inside your head. You are allowed only to state numbers, and your aim is to cultivate this form of noticing without judging. The real challenge is to extend it even into the moments when it **really** goes wrong, and when (in the old paradigm) you would have been tempted to use any means possible to get the horse's head down fast.

Instead of talking to yourself inside your head and absenting yourself from reality, use images which help you **influence** reality. Think of yourself as a suction device, perhaps some kind of limpet, that can draw the horse's back up. Or think of those machines they use to scrap old cars that have four massive arms, and that pick up the car and squash it into a rectangle. Your two 'arms' are your thighs (not your calves, as so many people think), and as they support your bodyweight and act as lever arms they pick up the horse underneath you. Remember how adults often pick up young children under the armpits, and imagine that if someone did that to you, the horse would be drawn up with you. Think of the push forward of your bear down becoming stronger than the horse's push back (see page 66), and bear down through the corridor made by your arms and the reins, thinking of pushing his neck and ears away from you.

Any words you say to yourself must be short reminders of positive points, said in a way you would like your teacher to say them to you. 'Bear down', 'breathe', 'keep kneeling', and 'that's it' are good examples, and the only negative comments you are allowed are 'lost it', 'whoops', 'd*≈n', 'b!*¿t', and a few other swear words. Some people's reminders tend to be about their body, like 'stay firm', 'keep the stretch', whilst others are about images, like 'limpet' or 'car grab'. Some people picture their images and do not need words at all. It is fine to use whatever style suits you best, as long as none of your comments, good or bad, ever becomes a soliloquy. Even 'inside leg on the girth; outside leg behind the girth; I must remember to keep the bend,' takes far too long to say (even if those words were helpful reminders, which I doubt). By the time you have finished your sentence you are half way down the next long side and have blinked and missed all of it!

Learning only takes place through paying attention, noticing differences, and putting two and two together as you work out what caused what. This creates a store of information in your brain's data bank, and enables you to create a map of how riding works. It is how you learned about your body and the world as a young child, and how the brain is designed to learn. With time and experience you expand that map – assuming, of course, that you do not fall into the trap of going round and round in circles making the same mistakes and practising doing it wrong. Your horse is there to help you teach yourself the cause-and-effect rules of riding so that you gradually expand this map. Unless you are a talented rider who has utilised this strategy unconsciously, there is no other way to learn.

■ *Troubleshooting – now*

Realise that your body is like a chain that is as strong as its weakest link, so when the horse hollows his back and makes a man-trap, you will give way in your weakest place (see illustrations overleaf). Some people collapse under their sternum and become 'C' shaped when he pushes back. Their backside tucks under too much, and their thighs rotate away from the saddle. Others fold at the hip joint, and their shoulders go forwards whilst their backside goes backwards as if into jumping position. Yet others hollow their back, so when their backside goes backwards they do not actually lean forwards but their front line lengthens. They may also grab on with their knees, and become too wide across the back. Some just topple back with their shoulders, so that there is still the same distance between their chin and the horse's ears. Which is your pattern? You need to know, so get external feedback if necessary to help you determine your weakest link.

Think of there being a right way for the horse and you to fit together, where your backside and his back both make a certain shape, matching like two pieces of a jigsaw puzzle. When the horse's back comes into the right shape, it is easy for you to fit into the right shape around him. But suppose that he wants to change the shape of his jigsaw puzzle piece. The path of least resistance is for you to collude with him, altering your shape to match his. All too easily, and perhaps without even knowing, you will give way at your weakest link and slide back down into the man-trap. But the challenge is to realise what is happening, and to refuse to play his game. By holding the shape of your jigsaw puzzle piece you make it impossible for him to change his. Then he fits around you, instead of you fitting around him.

When you are getting a good response from your horse, remind yourself to 'keep doing it, keep doing it', and this will help you appreciate that each moment is a time to 'do it' afresh. You cannot afford to take any time off from this process, which means that there is not even time for to you congratulate yourself when you have done well. The moment you think 'I did it!', you are assuming that since you have already arrived, you have no more need to journey. You are no longer riding your horse, but are **talking to yourself** about riding your horse. Whilst you might not appreciate the

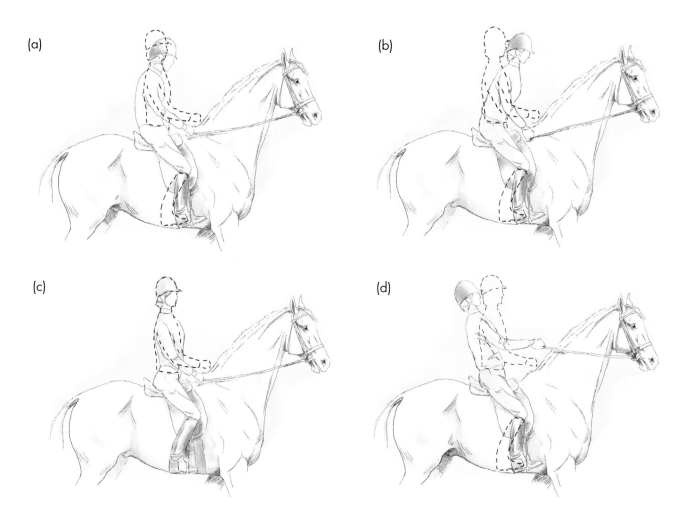

(a)

(b)

(c)

(d)

The rider's body is like a chain which gives way at its weakest link. So when the horse comes above the bit and 'pushes back' at the rider, she will: (a) give way under her sternum, rounding her back and pointing her seat bones forward; (b) close the hip joint, to fold towards jumping position; (c) hollow her back, so that her seat bones point back and slide back down the man-trap; or (d) topple back with her shoulders, thus keeping the same distance between her chin and his ears.

difference, your horse most certainly will. In fact, he probably knows more about what happens inside your head than you do. I hope you find this embarrassing enough to keep you motivated to **PAY ATTENTION**!

If you forget to be in process and get fixated on a certain outcome – which usually concerns getting the horse's head down – then again you have abandoned the learning process, becoming your own (and your horse's) worst enemy. If dressage judges, or even dressage arenas put you into this frame of mind, abandon competition or even schooling for a while, and use hacks to teach yourself how to remain in process, and pay attention. When all else fails, practise the pieces that constitute good riding – bearing down, plugging in, becoming narrow enough, supporting your bodyweight, etc. – and trust that the pay-off will come soon.

■ *Troubleshooting – on through time*

Once you have tasted success, you will almost inevitably want it again, and the day after the day you rode really well is usually disappointing. On the good day, it is as if you followed a certain recipe and baked a certain cake, and on the next day you just expect the cake to be there and are horribly upset when it isn't! So you become even more tempted to try and somehow create that end result by hook or by crook (which for most people means by pulling or fiddling). The reality is that you have to pay attention to the **means whereby** you created that result, so you have to put the same ingredients into the pot, and then mix them and bake them in the same way. The sad truth is that most of us want to arrive, and not to journey. But this desire spells the end of learning and of good, ethical riding, so at the end of a session when you have done well, catch yourself before you say 'I've got it, I've got it!' and cap your euphoria. Instead remind yourself that 'That will be an act to follow.' This may be a sobering thought, but it is a form of realism that protects you from the let-down that inevitably follows a blown-up vision of your triumph.

When you are riding well, do not let yourself float off on cloud nine. This may be tempting, but it is extremely limiting. Instead, ask yourself, 'How am I doing this?' Become aware of your body, find an image, and piece the recipe together. Remember that your aim is to be able to bake the same cake again tomorrow, but realise that realistically, it may take some time for you to discover all the ingredients in the recipe and to be able to reproduce that cake reliably. It may take you months to pin down the whole recipe, and you could be horribly thwarted by too much of one ingredient and not enough of another. Video feedback may help you iden-

Common responses

These vary from:

'I've no idea what shape his back is. It feels just like it always does.'

'Yes, I saw his head come up, but I've no idea what happened in his back.'

to:

'That's the first time I've ever felt that happen. His back came up! It really is a mound; he feels about a hand higher.'

'OK, I felt him hollow that time. My front gave way and I toppled back onto the back of my backside.'

'It's so hard not to react with my hand. I've tipped forward and begun to fiddle before I even realise it, and then of course I'm not in a position to bear down effectively and push his neck away from me.'

and:

'I can feel the whole thing with so much more subtlety now. If I change the angle of my pelvis even slightly I've lost him. Sometimes he's so quick that he catches me out, but usually I can feel the beginnings of the hollow and refuse to collude with him.'

tify the ways in which you have distorted the recipe, but with all the best will in the world, you may find that you completely lose that feeling, and discover it again only months or even years later. Become a recipe-sleuth, submit to this process, and enjoy it. If your only interest lies in consuming gourmet cakes, you will doom yourself to misery much of the time.

Realise that whilst riding and learning well, you are playing a game with your horse which I call the 'got it / lost it' game. The only thing that changes through time is the subtlety of the 'it' that you get and lose. Each time you 'get it' and each time you 'lose it' more information becomes available to your brain's data bank, and you etch in the map more deeply. Initially the game may go in fits and starts, and there may be plateaus where you cannot get any change to happen, so there is nothing to get, nothing to lose, and nothing to learn. The plateau is a sign that you are always doing the same thing in the same way, creating 'sameness' as the result, and since the brain learns by contrast, you have stymied yourself. The answer is to **do something different**, and if you do enough different things you will eventually hit on a recipe that works. The process can be quicker and easier, however, if you get help from outside. Do not let your plateaus last too long.

▪ *Test yourself – have you got it?*

People usually become aware of the moment in which things go right long before they become aware of the moment in which things go wrong. It is important to be able to make the correction that takes you from wrong to right; but you have not got it until you can feel that it is **about to go wrong**, and can prevent this from happening. (Ideally, of course, you never even get this far down the slippery slope of 'wrongness', and you catch the horse even before the idea of hollowing goes through his head. In fact, you ride him so well that the idea never **does** enter his head!) But given that it will, what is the first sign you get that things are about to go wrong? Do you see his head come up, or do you feel his back go down? You have not got it until you can feel changes in his back, and use those as your cue to respond. Can you find a correction appropriate to that first sign? Do you have to grope around for that correction, or do you find it quickly and easily? The smaller the mistake you correct, the smaller your correction, the less the horse is able to disorganise you, and the easier riding becomes.

You have got it when you can feel your horse's back come up, and when he feels as if he wants to reach away from you with his head and neck. This is a natural result of the change in his back, and if you feel (even slightly) that your hand needs to hold his head down and in place, you have not yet got it.

▪ *Off-horse exercise*

(I am indebted to equine sports massage therapist Pennie Hooper who invented the following exercise.)

Bend forward from the hips, so that your back is parallel to the floor. Then hollow your back, putting your chin up, and attempt to walk. You are now imitating a horse who is above the bit. You will find that you cannot take very long steps, and that the whole process is highly uncomfortable. Now imagine that your rider is hitting you with a whip, trying to make you more athletic, and realise that it is all but impossible to move any differently. Now tuck your chin in, imagining that she has put you in draw reins. Appreciate that your plight has become even worse.

Now bend forward from the hips but let your back round a bit. Bend your knees a bit, and let your chin drop naturally. When you walk like this, you will find that your movement is much freer, for the joints of your hind legs can articulate much more easily. Now, you can be a good athlete, but as soon as you hollow your back again your hind legs virtually lock up.

Realise from this that when the horse's back comes up, it is as if a space is created for his hind legs to step underneath him. With his back hollow, you could beat him black and blue, but he could not step under himself even if he wanted to. This means that as a rider, you have to be able to bring your horse's back up before you even think of making his hind legs step under him.

The Rider/Horse Partnership – An Overview of the Rider/Horse Interaction

▪ *Description of the ideal*

Good riders influence the horse through their alignment, and by bearing down, plugging in, supporting their own bodyweight, and using their thighs like levers. They can be likened to a martial artist not only in their body mechanics, but also in their philosophical stance, their mental focus, and their use of energy. They think of picking up the horse's energy and channelling it to their ends. They do not oppose his energy, or try to keep him so quiet and calm that they minimise his energy. They maintain a level of focus and intention that reads the horse from moment to moment, interacting with him to achieve a certain end.

Good riders are so quiet and still in their sitting that they **listen** to the horse instead of bombarding him with busy thoughts and body movements. Plugging in gives them a profound energetic connection with both his body and his mind, along with the ability to regulate his tempo. Their energetic connection with the horse enables them to 'take him' instead of having him 'take them'. In rising trot they enhance this connection by regulating its 'trampoline bounce', using their body mechanics to make the horse 'ping' in just the right way. They draw his back up instead of squashing it down, creating a push forward which is bigger than the horse's push back, and aiming that push through the corridor made by the lower arms and reins. By putting the lid on the end of the toothpaste tube they build up tone (or stuffing) within the horse's body. They keep him paying attention, and going forward so much that the energy flowing through the circuit is less likely to be lost or blocked.

Good riders are not wishy-washy in their body or their mind, and neither they, nor the average wishy-washy rider, have any idea of the depth and effect of this difference between them. Good riders make themselves able to match the power and energy of an animal who weighs over 1000lb. Despite appearances, and the descriptions they often give, they are not doing nothing.

■ *Common starting points*

Examples of these have been given in all of the previous sections, and whilst there are a number of common patterns, starting points are as many and varied as each individual. Much of the skill needed to work effectively with this book lies in diagnosing your own starting point. Few people take the time to do this in sufficient depth, and breakthroughs elude the many riders who do not appreciate the power of the present state. Only when you have **discovered what you are actually doing can you choose to do what you want**. Otherwise, the pattern that is ingrained in your neurology goes unrecognised by your conscious mind and maintains its power to run your behaviour. That 'Aha!' moment of recognition yields choice in what you do – as well as the need for 10,000 repetitions of the new co-ordination so that it becomes ingrained in your neurology as the new norm.

Most riders gloss over what is happening now, and instead of being here, they pretend that they are **there** – higher up the ladder, with more skills than they actually have. They want to ride movements that they do not yet have the knowledge to execute, and to ignore the cause-and-effect issues through which their biomechanics affect the horse's carriage. This is understandable in a paradigm where there is little on offer that makes 'here' a better place to be; but the problem is that you never actually leave 'here' when you pretend that you are 'there'. The only way to evolve out of 'here' is to **fully be here**, bringing in the awareness that shows you what you are doing, and gives you the chance to choose to do things differently.

The fix

Be prepared to go slowly. Crawl before you walk, and walk before you run. Build up your skills piece by piece, and take the time that it takes. Now that you have reached the end of this book go back to the beginning. Actually **do** the exercises; take the book to the stable yard and read parts of it before you ride. Keep them at the forefront of your mind, and set yourself a task for the day. Pair up with a friend and work together. Be systematic and thorough. Become recipe sleuths.

When the going gets tough, remember that each little breakthrough can make a world of difference. To an insecure rider, it is life-changing to feel more secure and capable. To an established rider with one or two fatal flaws, finding these is a triumph. Breakthroughs are each exciting on their own account, and that excitement mounts as they add up to the 'critical mass' of riding the horse in carriage. If you apply your time and your brain in productive ways, you can do it. I have yet to meet anyone who felt that the pay-off was not worth the effort.

Troubleshooting – now

It is a huge challenge to maintain the 'brain space' needed to juggle all of the pieces in the recipe, and to mix them all in the right order and the right proportions. Your brain will only be able to keep track of three or four pieces at once, but often, there must be more pieces in the recipe. Have a checklist and cycle through it. Keep a journal, and write notes to yourself. Use mental rehearsal (described in my previous books) to help you ingrain new patterns more quickly. Beware of amnesia – where you simply forget what you were working with – and beware of over-focus, where you try too hard and cannot see the wood for the trees. Stay aware of both the small pieces, and of how they come together to form the big picture. It is those big-picture pieces that often get forgotten – you might, for instance, forget that you must still ride your horse forward whilst you are paying attention to your breathing or your seat bones.

▪ *Troubleshooting – on through time*

Whatever your stage in riding, there is great power in realising that 'how' is the only missing element. This has been the missing piece in theories that describe perfection and then order you to do it, as if an act of will were the only requirement.

Common responses

These vary from:

'I'm still getting over the shock of all this. It's so unbelievable that mainstream thinking can be so unhelpful to riders like myself, and that I'm having to do virtually the opposite of everything I ever strived for.'

to:

'There are still some things that bug me about my riding, but nowhere near as much as there used to be.'

'It's as if I used to ride under an anaesthetic. I'm amazed by what I didn't notice happening.'

and:

'Now that my tool kit functions reasonably well I get much less frustrated with my horses and myself. It's such a joy to be able to love them when I'm riding as much as I love them from the ground.'

If you have been diagnosed as not having talent, or as being stiff, or inept in various other ways, this simply means that you are using the wrong 'how'. (It also means that your teachers were also using the wrong 'how', or they could have led you to the fix!) The right 'how' will solve your problems, and with the help of this book and some diligent work, you can find it. The basics that form the building blocks of skilled riding are laid out in these pages, and whilst 'back to basics' may be a rather hackneyed phrase, you now know what these basics are. You can use them to change your riding, and perhaps even your life.

Test yourself – have you got it?

You have got it when your learning process has become autonomous. As one discovery leads to another, it is as if you are following a thread that leads you through a maze of possibilities and shows you the right path. The thread becomes clearer and clearer as time goes by, and as you build on a more robust base of 'rightness'. Especially at first, you are bound to go up some blind alleys, and get lost from time to time. Get all the help that you can to get back on the not-straight-but-narrow path, and realise that as long as you learn from these mistakes, this time is not wasted.

Being on the track of your learning process means that you **cannot not** learn from your experiences with the horse. It does not mean that you are a perfect rider who knows everything, or that you do not need visual feedback or constructive help from the ground. It means that you are constantly paying attention, putting two and two together, and working out how riding works. This is the task that riding has become for you; its challenge and its joy lies here. You still have your blind spots – but you are in process, and you know it.

Off-horse exercises

Do your dismounted exercises again and again. You need awareness exercises, strengthening exercises, and stretching exercises. Join a Pilates class, a physioball class, a yoga class, a Tai Chi class, or any other class that supports your learning. Take Alexander or Feldenkrais lessons. Have regular bodywork. Look after your body – it's the greatest tool in your rider's tool kit.

Resources –
Addresses, Books, Videos, and Equipment

An 'Aids to Learning' catalogue and specific items listed below are available by post from:

Ride With Your Mind Products
Overdale Equestrian Centre
Nether Westcote
Chipping Norton
Oxon
OX7 6SD
UK

In the USA, the videotapes are available from:

Trafalgar Square Publishing
Howe Hill Road
North Pomfret
VT 05053
(800-423-4525)

For details of courses, products, etc. contact *www.mary-wanless.com*
This site has a link to an email discussion list for Ride With Your Mind at Yahoo! groups.

BOOKS

Learn With Your Mind by Mary Wanless, self-published by the author. A guide to learning for teachers and pupils; includes a list of Ride With Your Mind accredited coaches.

Ride With Your Mind: A Right-Brain Approach to Riding, Kenilworth Press. Available in the USA from Trafalgar Square Publishing, as *The Natural Rider.*

Ride With Your Mind Masterclass, from Kenilworth Press (UK) and Trafalgar Square Publishing (USA).

For the Good of the Horse, from Kenilworth Press (UK) and Trafalgar Square Publishing (USA).

For the Good of the Horse, from Kenilworth Press (UK) and Trafalgar Square Publishing (USA).

RIDE WITH YOUR MIND VIDEO
MASTERCLASS SERIES

Body Balance: The Basics – Gaining the equilibrium and proper body alignment necessary to establish riding skills which are biomechanically correct.

Rising Trot: Working on the Bit – Developing the correct interaction between rider and the horse, thus establishing the foundation for self-carriage.

Sitting Trot and Canter: Working on the Bit – How to develop correct use of the body and gain a truly independent seat.

Introducing Tempo, Transitions, Lengthening and Shortening of Stride – Tempo and the biomechanics of riding transitions, as well as lengthening and shortening of stride.

MARY WANLESS VIDEO MASTERCLASS SERIES

Symmetry and Circles – Correcting the problems inherent in turning and amplified by the asymmetries of the rider.

Introduction to Lateral Work – Discover the skills which enable riders to position their own and their horse's body with increasing precision.

Basic Principles…Advanced Movements – More advanced riders performing advanced movements as they rediscover the basic principles which are the foundation of riding.

A Rider's Guide to Body Awareness – The dynamics of riding explained using dismounted exercises which mimic the biomechanical challenges involved. Also shows some simple stretching exercises.

EQUIPMENT

Physioballs (also known as gymnasticballs) are an invaluable tool for developing balance and stability. Available in three sizes: *pony* (55cm diameter, suitable for riders up to 5ft), *thoroughbred* (65cm diameter, suitable for riders up to 5ft 6in.) and *warmblood* (75cm diameter, suitable for riders over 5ft 6in.). Available from Ride With Your Mind Products, physical therapists, fitness studios, and the internet.

Exercise band – heavy duty, 3ft stretchy rubber loop for strengthening abductor muscles. Available from Ride with Your Mind Products, physical therapists, fitness studios, etc.

The Rider's Belt – increases awareness of the pelvic area and helps the rider to learn to use her back effectively. Available only from from Ride With Your Mind Products, in two sizes: small (up to 38in. hip), and medium (over 38in. hip).

Pilates Fitness Circle – in the UK these can be purchased from Body Control Pilates Ltd (020 7379 3734 or www.bodycontrol.co.uk); in the USA from Stott Pilates (1-800-910-0001); or search the internet under 'Pilates'.

Thighmaster – available from department stores, fitness studios; or search the internet under 'Thighmaster'.

Glossary –
Ride With Your Mind Terms

Every subject has its own specialised vocabulary. This is not an attempt to be elitist: the vocabulary has arisen through our need to delineate various ideas more clearly than they are delineated within our conventional use of language. These terms (and others) are also used in the *Ride With Your Mind* books and also in *For the Good of the Rider*.

Within the glossary, words or phrases in *italics* refer to terms which are also listed.

'A' frame: the shape made by the rider's thigh bones as they hold the horse's ribcage in between them. It can help the rider to think of an imaginary point to the 'A' about 4 inches behind her backside. See also *'V' shape*.

alignment: the traditional shoulder/hip/heel vertical line. For 'hip' read the *greater trochanter of the femur*, i.e. the bony knobble at the top outside of the thigh, right on the line where your thigh becomes your pelvis. For 'heel' read the bony knobble on the side of the ankle.

asymmetries: neither rider nor horse is symmetrical. We all have our inherent asymmetry, and have to learn how to diagnose and work with it. Our quest is for functional symmetry, in which both sides of the body may need to do different things and feel different to get the net effect of symmetry.

balance point at the top of the rise: each rise must reach the point at which the rider could remain in balance over her feet without falling backwards or forwards.

bearing down: the action of the abdominal and back muscles which enables you to clear your throat. Good riders do this the whole time, but do not know that they do so. It requires *diaphragmatic breathing*. When the horse is working well, he too is bearing down.

'C' shaped: the shape of the front of the rider's body when it caves in. The rider's back is rounded, and her seat bones point forwards.

completing the circuit: concerns the flow of energy around an imaginary circuit which begins at the horse's hind legs, goes over his croup, and along the *long back muscles* which lie under the panels of the saddle. It continues up the crest of his neck to the poll and the mouth where it is received into the rein and the rider's hand. It then flows along her arm, into her back, and into the horse's back to refuel the circuit. There are many places in both the horse's and the rider's bodies where this energy flow can become blocked, or where the energy can be dissipated or dispersed. The horse is only correctly 'on the bit' or 'working over his back' when this circuit is complete. Only then can the rider perform correct *half-halts*.

correct bend: an elusive concept, often confused with a *jack-knife*. When the bend is correct, there is no 'break' at the wither. There is the illusion of a uniform curve from poll to tail, although this is not actually the case. In reality, the ribcage bulge is symmetrical, and both *long back muscles* can be felt equally clearly.

diaphragmatic breathing: the breathing pattern used by people who sing or play a wind instrument, and also by good riders who are *bearing down*. In contrast to upper-chest breathing, it brings the breath right down into the abdomen.

extension pattern: this is shown by both riders and horses when they lengthen the muscles of the abdomen and chest, and also the front/underside of the neck. The rider in extension pattern leans back, lifts her chest and chin, and usually ends up pulling on the reins and *water-skiing*. The horse in extension pattern comes above the bit. He then *lengthens his underside* in each step, and uses his forelegs to pull himself along. In the ideal movement pattern he *lengthens his top side*, reaching over his back and into the rein whilst pushing himself along from his hind legs. Horse and rider often mirror each other in this pattern, and either one can trigger it in the other. Extension pattern is the opposite of *flexion pattern*.

first tool kit: the rider's body, and how she affects the horse simply by how she sits on him. Key factors in this are her *alignment*, her *muscle tone*, the way in which she uses her thigh as a *lever*, and her ability to *match the forces which the horse's movement exerts on her body*.

flexion pattern: this is the opposite of *extension pattern*. The horse lengthens his top line, and raises his back. He concurrently shortens his abdominal muscles, so instead of hanging down, they are used to support his back. He can then push himself along from his hind legs, bring them more underneath him, and flex his hocks. (To understand this in practice, stand up, hollow your back and attempt to hug one knee. Then take the hollow out of your back and realise that you can bring your knee much closer to your chest.) The rider in flexion pattern remains vertical and does not allow the muscles of her front to lengthen. She also has her *front tendons* popped up.

front tendons: the tendons of the quadriceps muscle group which forms the front of the thigh. If you put your fingers in the angle between your thigh and your torso and then lift your knee, you can feel these tendons stick up. They need to do this when you are riding.

greater trochanter of the femur: the bony knobble at the top outside of the thigh. Eleven muscles attach into this, and it is a very important landmark. Also known as the stabiliser.

growing tall: this happens when the rider lifts her ribs up away from her hips. Although many riders think this is the right thing to do, it stops them from having the stable, centred stance of a martial artist. It hollows the rider's back, makes her breathe only in her upper chest, and stops her from *bearing down*. It also puts her into *extension pattern*.

half-halt: the Mecca of riding! It happens in one down beat, and sits the horse down. It has nothing to do with leaning back, *growing tall*, *water-skiing*, or pulling on the reins. Many people attempt to ride half-halts when they do not yet have the *circuit complete*. Without this, the half-halt cannot 'go through'. It is better not to attempt to ride half-halts until they start happening by accident, as a by-product of the rider's position corrections.

half-haul: this is what actually happens to most people when they attempt a *half-halt*.

horse taking the rider: this happens when the rider has lost control of the tempo. It is similar to riding a bicycle, going down hill, and finding that you can no longer pedal fast enough to keep up.

isometric muscle use: in this the muscle contracts but does not shorten. The muscle works at high *muscle tone*, and this gives the rider stability and body control. To understand this, think of the difference between the movement of a dancer or a gymnast - who both have high tone - and that of a drunk, who has extremely low tone. Riding is a dynamic isometric skill, in which the rider gains stability by pitting opposing muscle groups against each other. Isometric contraction happens when you push against a resistance you cannot move, e.g. if you attempt to push a wardrobe. As another example, sit in a chair and attempt to lift one knee whilst you simultaneously put one hand on that knee and hold it down. You will use your front thigh muscles (the quadriceps group) isometrically and will also *pop* your *front tendons*.

jack-knife: a turn in which the horse's wither falls to the outside as the rider brings the horse's nose to the inside. Many riders mistake a jack-knife for a *correct bend*.

lace up across the back: an image which helps riders to 'switch on' the muscles of the lower back, as if you were laced into a corset which pulled both sides of the back in towards the middle. It is a feeling which makes you *narrower*, and is another way of talking about the '*pinch*'.

lateral 'C' curve: an asymmetrical pattern in which the rider's upper body curves to the side. This usually happens on one rein, and her head is displaced to the inside of the circle. She has a lower inside shoulder and creases in the region of her waistband. Either seat bone may have become heavier, whilst the other becomes lighter or disappears.

left-brain hemisphere: the side of the brain which understands language, and processes information linearly. Thus it adds letters together to make words, and puts words together to make sentences. It can read and understand books on riding and knows what should be happening; but it does not organise the body and ride the horse. Riding itself is a *right-brain* skill.

lengthening the top side: the movement pattern in which the horse stretches along his top line with every step he takes. The muscles of his underneath (i.e. his flexor muscles) stay short, and he can bring his hind legs underneath him. This is the same as *flexion pattern*.

lengthening the underside: the movement pattern in which the horse pulls himself along with his front legs and lengthens the underside of his body in each step. This is the same as extension pattern.

leverage: when the rider sits well, the thigh is used as a lever. The front thigh muscles (the quadriceps group) work in the same way that they do if you stand in an 'on-horse' position. Doing this will soon make the muscles hurt because of the way in which they are counterbalancing your bodyweight. Using your front thigh muscles well when you ride helps you to keep your weight out of the horse's *man-trap* and to create the *suction* which can lift his back.

long back muscle: the muscle which lies beneath the panel of the saddle on each side of the horse's spine.

lumbar spine: the part of the spine between the ribs and the hips. Although many riders 'give' here in sitting trot, the best riders do not 'wiggle in the middle'. Instead they stay 'with' the horse by giving in the hip joints. The lumbar spine is not designed to be used as a joint. *Bearing down* helps to hold it stable.

man-trap: the hollow of the horse's back. If the rider presses her weight down into the man-trap, the horse's back will become hollow. By using her thigh to create *leverage*, the rider counterbalances the weight of her upper body, and stops her weight from falling into the man-trap. By doing this she can generate suction and can actually lift his back.

matching the forces which the horse's movement exerts on your body: this is the fundamental challenge of riding. Only then can you stay 'with' the horse in each step. If you do not do this you will bump backwards in sitting trot and/or pull back on the reins in an attempt to stabilise yourself. Matching those forces is not the same as relaxing. It is because of the need to do this that riding is a dynamic *isometric* skill, requiring high *muscle tone*. In rising trot the swing forward of the pelvis must match the thrust of the horse's hind leg, and bring the rider to the *balance point*.

muscle tone: the texture of the body, i.e. the firmness of the muscles. On average, men have 35 per cent higher muscle tone than women, and this makes their muscles less 'floppy', and more firm. The ideal texture is like putty, as opposed to jelly. Having naturally high tone makes the rider much more stable, and makes riding much easier. Low-tone riders improve a lot as they increase their tone, and discover how to 'switch on' their muscles isometrically.

narrowness, or narrowing in: the quality of becoming narrower from side to side, and another term for the '*pinch*'. The increased muscle tone of *lacing up across the back* helps in this. In effect, humans are too wide for horses, and we have to narrow in so that the *neck of the femur* can lie across the horse's *long back muscle* on each side. Usually, only one of these is in place, whilst the other one has fallen off the back muscle. This goes a long way to explaining why it is that so many of us ride much better on one rein than we do on the other.

neck of the femur: at the knobble of the *greater trochanter* the thigh bone turns inwards, forming the neck of the femur, and then the ball which fits into the socket of the hip joint. The neck of the femur ideally lies across the horse's long back muscle on each side.

neutral spine: the ideal way of sitting in which the rider's spinal curves are balanced, and her seat bones point down. She is neither hollow-backed, which makes them point backwards, nor round-backed, which makes them point forwards. In this position her spine is best placed to withstand the forces acting on it, and she can stabilise her *lumbar spine*. Many riders who have back pain become pain-free once they come into neutral spine.

pinch: I use this term less than I used to, since the word has been traditionally used by Americans for another function, and this caused confusion. It is essentially the same as *narrowing in* and *lacing up across the back*.

plugging in: reducing the amount of movement in each seat bone so that you do not shove with your backside. The seat-bone movement matches the amount of movement in the horse's long back muscle.

popping tendons: when you stick out the tendons at the front of the thigh, behind the knee, and around the ankle, you have a way of increasing the *muscle tone* of the thigh and calf. This helps to stabilise the lower leg.

pushing a baby buggy: the attitude of the hand when the rider is pushing it forward instead of pulling back.

pushing forward from your back: or beginning your *bear down* in your back. Using the lower back muscles *isometrically*, so that they help the rider to generate the forward force which keeps her 'with' the horse, and able to *match the forces which his movement exerts on her body*.

rider taking the horse: the rider is in control of tempo. This is like riding a bicycle, pushing the pedals round, and being in control of the speed at which the wheels go round. In a similar way, the rider controls the speed of the horse's legs.

right-brain hemisphere: the side of the brain which does not have access to language. It processes information as a whole (instead of in parts like the *left-brain hemisphere*), and is used in solving spatial and visual problems, e.g. putting on a cardigan, riding, recognising faces. It thinks by using visual images, and 'feelages'.

second tool kit: working with the school movements, using them to set gymnastic challenges. This is most beneficial when the rider's *first tool kit* is working well.

stuffing: another word for *muscle tone*. High tone makes the horse like a brand new stuffed toy horse, low tone makes him like an elderly one which has seen better days. The high-tone horse is 'bursting out of his skin' and probably also 'full of himself'. Being highly stuffed gives the rider the high tone of Superman, instead of the low tone of Clark Kent. A highly toned rider sits very still, and we commonly attribute her lack of wobbles, wiggles and bumps to her level of relaxation and not to her high muscle tone.

suction: the ability to lift the horse's back by using the thigh as a lever. Doing this helps to ensure that you will not push his back down by falling back down the *mantrap*.

supporting your own bodyweight: sitting lightly, and using the thigh as a *lever* so that you do not become a dead weight down the horse's *man-trap*.

turning like a bus: a correct turn in which the rider controls the horse's forehand and he does not *jack-knife*. The turn is reminiscent of a turn about the haunches. Buses do not articulate like lorries, hence thinking like this helps to stop the *jack-knife*.

'V' shape: the shape made by the rider's thighs as they hold the horse's ribcage between them. See also *'A' frame*.

water-skiing: a description of the rider who leans back, and pulls on the reins whilst pushing into the stirrups, as if she were being towed along by a motor boat. She probably also *grows tall*, lengthening her front to show *extension pattern*.

whole brain knowing: the ability to link feelings with words, so that you can explain in language the coordinations of riding. This can only be done by a rider with high awareness, who has experienced a lot of contrasts in her learning. As a result of this, she knows in language what she knows in feels.

Index

Page numbers in **bold** refer to illustrations.